WE CAN NEGOTIATE TOO!

Negotiation skills for young minds

ANUJ JAGANNATHAN

Dedicated to my family who have been a constant support throughout my life. My parents are both academicians, successful authors and a major inspiration. My wife and daughters provide the encouragement and motivation for all my endeavors.

WE CAN NEGOTIATE TOO!

PREFACE

Hello, my young readers! I am glad you decided to read this book. There are many books on negotiation. But this book is different! It is my effort to introduce this key topic to kids and young adults. We all negotiate daily. Kids are born negotiators and start practicing this skill early in life. However, at this stage it is an intuitive approach. This is an essential skill for everybody to study and enhance, more so for kids and young adults!

Negotiation is not limited only to professionals or those in business. Kids and young adults have frequent negotiations with parents, friends, family, teachers, and others. Do you remember the time when you wanted the beautiful doll or the Lego set? How about the time when you wanted to pursue a course of your dreams and had to negotiate with your parents? I will present the details of this skill to build the interest in this topic among young readers.

The benefits of negotiation can add up over a long time. So, as a kid or young adult, if you can learn the skills to negotiate effectively at an early age, you can reap benefits for the rest of your lives. You should note that negotiation is not about the best deal or a winning proposal for one party. It is all about the best outcome that provides a feeling of satisfaction to both or all parties involved.

It is my promise that by the time you finish reading the book, you would have added several tips and tricks to your toolkit to deal with common negotiation situations you face. These points will help you become a better negotiator. You will see a lot of examples and daily life experiences from personal life as well as from friends and family members. While it is important to learn from successful negotiation stories that share some smart strategies and generate a positive feeling, we can also learn from situations where the negotiation did not go well. Right? So, I will share many such cases that help you to deal with negotiations that did not go as planned. You can find out after reading this book what went wrong and how to avoid making such mistakes. The psychology of influencing works differently with kids and young adults, and it is valuable to understand the psychology for your negotiations.

After my first book *Negotiation Quotient* was published in 2019, I told my friends that my next book will be for kids and young adults to help them understand and become better at negotiation, and they agreed it was a great idea. I sent out surveys to connections and friends asking them the simple question: Should kids and young adults learn/study negotiation early in life? Answer was a big YES.

Negotiation is a skill that everybody needs but it is not taught to everybody. Kids and young adults, of course, are not taught this skill at school or college level. In private forums, I note a lot of discussion about teaching kids and young adults leadership and other skills that they need in their life. I think negotiation is definitely one of these skills.

The family environment is a big source of negotiation practices. In families, kids and young adults learn negotiation by observing parent(s) and other family members, but they do not understand why certain negotiating actions are taken, unless they are specifically taught the strategy behind the actions.

My young readers, you will gain significantly from this book, and will be able to apply everything you learned from this book in your day-to-day negotiations. Remember, next time when you negotiate with your friends, siblings or parents, some of the points in this book will come in handy. I am sure this book will be your companion to help you navigate through all types of negotiations.

Now, for the parents, the value of this book is that they will understand a bit more about negotiating with kids, and since the book primarily focusses on a win-win scenario, the parents will benefit from the skills that children learn by reading here. Parents will also be happy and proud to recognize the value that the kids can generate over their lifetime by developing proper negotiation skills.

Okay my young readers, are you now ready to dive into the book and learn more? Are you interested in improving your negotiation skills? Let's go!

CONTENTS

CHAPTER 1
INTRODUCTION

L et's start this chapter with a negotiation story. What do you do when you want to negotiate with your parents for a birthday gift? This is the example of a letter that Rahul, a nine-year-old boy, wrote to his parents a few days before his birthday. He presented a list of five gift options, including a picture for each:

- Disney+ subscription for one year;
- Water slide for swimming pool at home;
- Fish tank;
- Monkey bars over the swimming pool; and
- A cruise vacation

Image 1 - Rahul handing out a letter to his parents

Now, Rahul's primary objective was to get a Disney+ subscription. However, he knew that he had to provide a few gift options, and build in some likely and not-so-likely options. Of the list, he already knew that his parents would rule out the waterslide, monkey bars, and cruise vacation straightaway. We see the effect of High value-Low value strategy here (I will explain more about this strategy in Chapter 3). Eventually, it came down to Disney+ and the fish tank.

At his age, Rahul did a great job sharing his interests as a preparation for negotiation. Moreover, to close the deal, he provided a box for his parents to write the selected gift option and sign. In the next few chapters, we will talk more about his approach, and I will highlight strategies that he could have utilized differently. So, remember to follow along the story of Rahul.

This is one example of a negotiation that we all will likely face on a regular basis. Many such negotiation situations come our way every day, and it is important how we act in the most effective manner. The objective is to achieve the desired results, keeping in mind the interests of all parties involved in the negotiation.

It is fascinating to see the negotiation skills children use at a very young age. Many of the strategies and techniques that kids and young adults utilize are intuitive. Gradually, they give up those skills as they grow older. Until the age of around eight, children use emotional methods to gain a favorable response in negotiation with parents, but such methods might not work if the children are dealing with siblings or friends. As a result, a young negotiator is at a loss on what to do if the emotional methods don't work. As per the work of experts Dr. Theodore Shapiro and Dr. Richard Perry, around eight years kids enter the age of thinking and reasoning. This is the age where they develop the intellect and begin to make rational choices. So, at this age you see children move away from a negotiation strategy emphasizing emotions to a more thoughtful and logical negotiation style. Often, kids at this age provide reasoning, ask the right questions, and demand justification. For example, an eight-year-old kid once asked his father, "Daddy, is $5 a lot of money?"

The dad replied, "No it is not."

This answer triggered the son to ask the next logical question, "Then I am sure you could buy this toy car for me. It costs only $5!"

When I provide negotiation training to participants, I ask one question: "So, how many of you have attended a class or read about negotiation?" Typically, a small percentage of the class raises their hand in response to the question. Despite negotiation being one of the most commonly used skills in everyday life, people do not learn or read about developing or enhancing negotiation skills from an early age. They are expected to walk into negotiations and instinctively handle the situation. Kids and young adults start negotiating at a very early age with friends and family, but since they are not taught proper negotiation practices, they only apply what they have observed or what comes to them naturally and intuitively.

The essential skills that we normally learn later in life must be introduced early in life. In one personal instance at the age of twenty-six, I would have received at least an additional $5,000 in a deal, if I had negotiated adequately. I left this value on the table. And note that this is just one instance. Now, think of multiple such decisions you have to make over a lifetime. Imagine the value that you can generate over multiple transactions, and how much that would grow over the course of your life.

I believe it is critical for each of you, my young readers, to improve your negotiating abilities. After all, this is one of the most basic skills that you need daily. Remember the last time you wanted something from your parents, and wished that you knew the best way to get it? In this book, you will learn important points and tips to help you toward becoming a better negotiator. My daughter was talking to her friend and asked me a question: "Papa, what should we do in this situation?" I explained what the situation needs in terms of negotiation. Upon understanding, she said, "I am getting better at negotiating!"

As I was writing this section, my daughter said to me, "I'm bored! What should I do?" She had received a digital ban for twenty-four hours. Have you ever been in a similar situation?

"Go and negotiate with Mom! Explain to her how and why you would like to use your digital time. It should be something meaningful such as reading a book, something that will get a positive response. And also commit to a specific time limit," I suggested.

A little while later, she came back and said, "OK, I can now have the tablet!" She had done exactly what I told her, and also completed a chore that her mom asked her to do. It was a win-win situation for both of them.

Applying the art and science of negotiation has helped me develop the necessary skills to become a better negotiator. This book will help you understand the regular negotiation practices, along with the behaviors and techniques, that make your negotiations effective. If you understand all the points explained and follow the approach in this book, you will be able to apply them in any of your negotiations. Consistently keeping the skills at the back of your mind and analyzing how you can use them will lead to a successful application.

At the end of the book, you will find a checklist to serve as a guide when you negotiate. Check off the boxes on the checklist (as applicable) and consult the book for more info to help you succeed in negotiations.

CHAPTER 2
THE SCIENCE AND ART OF NEGOTIATION

Do you find the negotiation process challenging or intriguing? Does the word "negotiation" scare you because you think you don't know how to handle it?

This chapter is an overview that I call "The Science and Art of Negotiation." Negotiation is a three-phase process which is the "science of negotiation." The "art of negotiation" refers to the correct behaviors and techniques that support the process. Let me explain the science and art of negotiation using something that is closer to your heart. Do you like pizza, garlic bread and soda? I know all my young readers do. We can associate the pizza as the science, and the garlic bread and soda as the art of negotiation. Let me discuss further.

Would it be a good meal if there was only pizza, without garlic bread or soda? No. The pizza is supported by the garlic bread and soda to make it a satisfying meal. Similarly, the science (three-phase process) and art (appropriate behaviors and effective techniques) of negotiation have to go together, to make the negotiation successful.

Before we move forward to discuss the process of negotiation, let's understand what negotiation is. In my workshops, people frequently say negotiation means "win-win," "coming to a compromise," or "building trust." However, I sometimes also hear "proving your point" or "making sure I win." Are these answers correct? They might be correct depending on the situation, and the type of negotiation. Negotiations happen when the parties have different goals. So, in general, you would try to achieve the best results from the negotiation, not only for yourself but also for the other party. Here is my definition of negotiation:

> *Negotiation is an interaction between two or more parties to get expected results, both for themselves and for the other party or parties*

Now let's break this down and analyze this definition of negotiation in a bit more detail.

- Negotiation is an interaction between two or more persons such as parents, grandparents, siblings, friends, etc. This exchange is important to establish the connection in a negotiation, and it is usually done face-to-face with the other person. However, in some cases, it could take place remotely on phone, video, or online (that I call "click-thru negotiation", discussed in Chapter 3).

- Achieving results for *both or all* parties should be the goal of every negotiation. Remember, it is not only about you. You have to think about the other party, too. If you are negotiating with a friend, sibling or parent, understand what they need.

Let's note some key points about negotiations:

- Negotiation is everywhere and we are already negotiators. We negotiate multiple times, and under different circumstances, in a single day. We probably don't even realize that we are practicing it. Negotiating starts very early in life. Babies and little kids negotiate, too. Based on the circumstances, their approach to negotiating might be limited to emotional methods such as yelling, crying, or wailing. As they grow older, kids begin utilizing negotiation strategies based on their intuition, but these might not work in every situation. As mentioned in the previous chapter, around the age of eight, kids start thinking with reasoning. It is important to keep improving negotiating abilities by developing better skills through learning and experience.

- We all have different styles, and our negotiation skills and strategies depend on our individual style. Improving our approach to negotiation is a continuous learning process, including understanding our own style and molding it over time, as per the situation and circumstance. We will discuss styles in more detail in Chapter 4.

- Negotiation needs an open mind. Not all negotiations go as you expect. It is very important to remember that in some situations, your negotiation might fail and either party could walk away if they are not able to get the result they want. If you want to be a good negotiator, you should not feel bad about a failure in negotiation and decide when it is a good time to stop. However, a good understanding of the skills and techniques, and consistent practice will help polish the negotiation skills. Further, you learn every time you negotiate. The more you practice, the better you will get at negotiating. Remember, practice makes you perfect! As with anything else you do, the best results come when you put in the effort and enjoy the process.

Science of negotiation

The science of negotiation refers to the three phases of the negotiation process: Prepare, Engage and Close. All three phases play an equally critical role in the negotiation.

Prepare: In this phase, important information is gathered, and a plan is made to engage in the negotiation. Just like other aspects of life where proper planning and assembling of available facts plays a key role in the success of our efforts, negotiation success is heavily dependent on the preparation that goes into the start of the negotiation. Even skilled negotiators need to put in adequate time and effort in preparation as every case is different and has to be dealt with accordingly.

Engage: Here one interacts with the other person in a negotiation. All the preparation needs to be backed up by a proper delivery of the information to the other party, or parties, in the negotiation. Solid preparation helps with the actual engagement in a negotiation. This phase is to interact properly with the other party, depending on the circumstances.

Close: This final phase is when the agreement is achieved, and the deal is sealed to get the benefit of the hard work from preparation and engagement. No negotiation is final unless it is properly closed. If a decision needs to be approved by somebody to be final, this is the phase to get that approval.

Art of negotiation

Behaviors and influencing techniques are essential all through and adequately support the entire negotiation process. They represent the art of negotiation. It is vital to strike the right balance between the phases of negotiation, and the appropriate use of behaviors and techniques.

In each of the three phases, the behaviors and techniques should be used properly to have a successful negotiation.

· · ·

The overall negotiation process is a proper balance of the science and the art. This blend results in the development of your negotiating ability. In the next two chapters, we will dive deeper into the science and the art that are key to the whole process. I know you all like stories. We will look at negotiation via examples and stories that you all can relate to. These stories happen very regularly in our day-to-day life. After reading these stories, you will think, "This has happened to me before!"

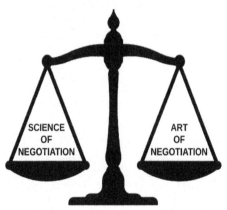

Image 2 - Balance of Negotiation

CHAPTER 3
THE SCIENCE OF NEGOTIATION

Concepts and terms explained in this chapter

PREPARE PHASE:

WHAM Strategy- What, How and More Strategy to explain the benefits and value that your item or your proposal provides to the other party.

Position - A person's point of view that is the basis of the negotiation.

Interest - The actual reasons behind the person's position.

Base Level - It is the base point to enable a person to make a decision.

Alternatives - The "Plan B" if the negotiation is not successful.

TRAIN – This is the best alternative a person has if the negotiation is not successful (Top Ranked Alternative in Negotiation).

Types of Negotiations – The various types of negotiations that require different strategies.

ENGAGE PHASE:

Conduct – Key attributes you need to have in a negotiation.

Presenting your point – Highlights the most effective way to present your point to get positive results.

Anchoring – This is the starting point for any of the parties in the negotiation when it involves a number (quantity, price, etc.)

CLOSE PHASE:

Agreement – Final agreement from all the necessary people on the points discussed during the negotiation.

Record – Recording all the agreed points on paper or other electronic way.

Handshake – Final closure of all agreed points by signing or via confirmation email.

• • •

Let's dive deeper into the Science of Negotiation. Remember this is the pizza as per the explanation in the previous chapter. There are three phases in the science of negotiation:

> Phase 1 – Prepare
>
> Phase 2 – Engage
>
> Phase 3 – Close

Now we will explore these three phases in detail.

· · ·

PHASE 1: PREPARE

When you have to submit a project about a topic, what do you do? You first research and prepare for the project, correct? Yes, you do, and the same applies to your negotiations. In this initial phase of negotiation, it is essential to prepare well for your negotiations by knowing what you can offer, what your interests are, and what the other party's interests are.

There is a saying: *"If you fail to prepare properly, then you are preparing to fail"*. The Prepare phase is a crucial phase where you *plan* for the negotiation. Strong preparation will also make you more confident.

For preparation to help result in an effective negotiation, there are some major points to note that we will explore ahead.

WHAT, HOW AND MORE (WHAM) Strategy

In the Prepare phase, it is necessary to show the importance of the item that you are providing or the idea that you are proposing.

Let me introduce an effective strategy that will lead the way to success in your negotiation. Whenever you want to showcase your item or idea to the other party, you can apply the **WHAM** (What, How And More) **Strategy**. This acronym also stands for Winning Heart And Mind (WHAM), which means that when you are preparing for your negotiation, it is important to consider winning the heart and mind of the other person to convince him/her. The "What" and "How" will win the other person's mind, and the "More" will win the other person's heart.

Let's now understand the three parts with examples.

What

The first part is to state clearly the "what" in your negotiation, meaning it could be an item you are offering, an idea you are proposing or a point you are trying to make. Also, it is key to highlight how it will benefit the other person.

Let's look at an example: Do you negotiate with a parent for additional screen time (TV, videogame, or any other device)? In order to support your idea to get additional screen time, you need to mention what you can do to get the screen time. Can you do some chores or additional studies? This is your "What". Clearly, if you do the chores or the additional studies, it benefits the parent or considers the parent's interests too.

Do you remember Rahul's story from Chapter 1? He was negotiating with his parents for his birthday gift. He wanted to share his gift ideas with his parents. So, for the "what" he prepared a list of five gift ideas. It was an important step in preparation for him to narrow down to his "what." Now, it would have been even better if he highlighted how the items were good for the parents or the family.

How

The second part of the WHAM strategy presents the uniqueness or the "how" of your item or what your idea is, i.e., a different way to support the "what". This part is important because it highlights how your "What" is special.

Going back to the earlier example of requesting additional screen time, in the "What" you state what you can do such as chores or additional studies. So, in the "How" you can support your idea and make it unique. Some of the ways to make your proposal more interesting and special are:

- Prepare rules for what chores you will do and how much screen time you will get, and make a schedule for the chores and screen time. This will make your proposal more appealing to the parent.

- Make your idea better by saying you will do chores before you get screen time. Some kids say they will do the chores after the screen time. Are you one of those kids? You will win your parents' attention if you specifically agree to do the chores before.

- Prove your dedication or demonstrate speed. If you can do the additional studies quickly in thirty minutes, for instance, you can get more screen time than agreed.

Back to Rahul. He prepared a list of five gift ideas. That was his "what" of the idea. To support the "what" he did some research online and pulled some pictures to support each of the five gift ideas. This was a very clever way to highlight his idea. Do you agree?

More

This last part of your preparation strategy refers to how you can give "more" to convince the other person about your idea and make your negotiation run smoothly. Remember that "what" and "how" win the mind but "more" wins the heart. By adding something more, you can give more value to the other party in the negotiation. For example, value can be created in a negotiation by extending attractive discounts or giving away some products or services.

To close on the earlier example on additional screen time, you could win the heart if you agreed to the additional studies and chores. Further, if you have a younger sibling, you could propose to help the younger sibling with his/her studies. Anything you do more will give you better negotiating power.

Now, to wrap up the WHAM strategy for Rahul's story, he presented his ideas and also added pictures to support his ideas. To do even more, he could help his parents by identifying where his gift items were available at a good price. If he had done all the homework to get the links and best price, it would make it easier for his parents, and ensure the negotiation runs smoothly.

Do you think you will now be able to apply the WHAM strategy to win the heart and mind of the other person? Practice this regularly, write it down and you will soon master this strategy. It is powerful and you can apply it in most situations. Give it a go.

In the next two sections, we will discuss two vital elements of the Prepare phase - (1) List your interests, and (2) Know your alternatives.

List your interests

Let's first discuss two different methods to negotiate:

(1)   First method to negotiate is *"self-interest"*. This means that when two people negotiate for something, they both state what they need, and focus on their needs during the negotiation. They want to achieve their own interests. In these cases, they have to make a quick decision. In general, kids and young adults are good at making such decisions. As an example, my younger daughter was reading on the laptop when I asked her to stop. Immediately, she mentioned that she would stop as soon as the older daughter stopped using her phone. It was a quick exchange, and I agreed, as it was fair.

You need to be careful of some tactics that are used in this method of negotiations. The other party or person might expect a lot or try to shortchange you. I talked to a mother whose son exchanges Pokémon cards with other children. She explained that every time he exchanged cards, he would give away "popular" cards in exchange for not-so-good ones. This can be avoided by being aware of these tactics, and asking the other person to negotiate with a different method called "joint interests."

(2) *"Joint-interests"* is a method to work with the other person to satisfy the interests of both or all. More effort is required to build a good relationship, partnership, and under- standing with the other person. You have to think and prepare very well for these types of negotiations. All the parties need to feel that it was a win-win (win for all).

In some cases, self-interest negotiation might work well, but, in reality, joint-interests is the most common and effective method in negotiations. In this book, we will look at many examples of joint interests. If you are planning to negotiate with the other person, understand which method will be best to use in negotiation.

Let's delve into the joint-interests method in a bit more detail by explaining **Positions** and **Interests.** Here is a simple example to explain these:

A mother and her daughter are negotiating about the daughter joining a swimming class. As you know, when a child starts to learn swimming, he or she is likely scared of the unknown. In this instance, let's look at what are the *Positions* and *Interests*.

Positions: This is the point of view of the daughter or mother. The daughter's position is that she does not want to go swimming and the mother's position is that she wants the daughter to join the class. Positions are the primary reasons for a negotiation. So, this is what they want.

Interests: Now, it is important to understand that both the mother and her daughter have some interests behind their positions. The mother mentions her interests that swimming is a life-saving skill, good exercise and lots of fun. She wants her daughter to learn swimming and be able to enjoy it with family and friends. After discussing further with the daughter, the mother understands her interests, namely that she is scared of deep water, does not want to learn with many other kids, the water is cold, etc. This is to say why they want it.

Analyzing the above example, both mother and child have valid interests but they must listen to the other's interests as well. In this case, both the child and mother will have to understand and appreciate each other's interests to achieve a win–win. This is vital in the joint-interest method of negotiation.

This simple example clearly provides the distinction between *Positions* and *Interests*. Negotiating over positions is ineffective, often resulting in a compromise or a walk away. In other words, the result might not be what either party wants. On the other hand, negotiating with interests in mind often results in positive results and mutual gains.

People often ask me: "What is one thing that you would like to mention that people should know about negotiation?" While there are several aspects that contribute to a successful negotiation, of prime importance is the ability to focus on interests. A primary objective is not only to know our own interests but also to understand the other party's interests. Understanding interests also helps to build a good relationship.

To understand interests better, the parties have to be honest and open to discussing possible solutions beyond the positions in the negotiation. They should also clearly discuss any differences in opinion so that they are fully aware of challenges. In a negotiation, where the interests of one person cannot be met, proper reasons should be explained as to why they cannot be met, so that good relationships remain intact.

A classic illustration of Positions and Interests well known around the world is the story of the two sisters and an orange. Although there are several versions of the story, the main point of the story centers around the concept of Interests in a negotiation.

Two sisters were arguing over who would get the last remaining orange. In this case, the mother made an agreement to split the orange in half so that both daughters would get a fair share. So, was this a "win-win" situation? Many people would say "Yes" because both got half of the orange. But, the answer is "No." It was just a compromise. The point of this story is beyond the compromise. The story is about understanding the interests of the sisters. As it turns out, one sister wanted to eat the fruit and the other wanted the peel to bake a cake. If an attempt was made to find out what each sister wanted to do with the orange prior to the compromise, the interests of each of the sisters could have been achieved and truly have resulted in a "win-win".

A colleague of mine complained that she regularly has to negotiate with her kids, and it is challenging as they always keep asking for something more. I suggested that if she were having a similar discussion with adults, she likely would do everything to understand the interests of people, and come to a solution that worked for all parties. So, why would she not do that with her kids? After all, it is also a negotiation and the same principles apply. She should consider the interests of the kids and build solutions which mutually benefit her kids and herself.

Going back to Rahul's negotiation with his parents for his birthday gift. This was an example of negotiation where he needed to invest time to understand the parent's interests and keep in mind both his own interests and those of his parents to make it a successful negotiation. He should prepare to highlight to his parents what he can do for them.

So, what do you need to do to understand interests? You need to put in a specific effort to assess the other party's interests. The following actions are helpful in this process:

- Believe that a win-win is possible and stretch your imagination to find beneficial solutions for all;
- List down your interests and theirs and make a list of multiple interests from understanding of objectives;
- Determine the key decision-maker on their side to cater to his/her interests; and
- Assess if any interests or positions of the other person could create conflict and disagreement, and prepare solutions to handle those.

In the Engage phase, you would further explore and confirm the other party's interests which might not be clearly specified, and by doing so, build solutions for the implied interests.

Now to support the topic of interests a bit further, let's look at some interesting stories.

I am sure you all have been to IKEA. Am I right?

This is a story from the small town of Dublin in California, U.S.A. After years of negotiations, the IKEA store in Dublin is expected to become a reality with a city council approval received in November 2018. The planned 317,000-square-foot store on a 27-acre site is expected to be ready in three years.

Along the long and difficult path to City approval, IKEA faced challenges from the city's residents. Concerns were mostly around the store's appearance and its impact on convenience, including traffic, vast parking lots that could appear in front of the store, and the dominant blue and yellow colors. As a result, IKEA made it a priority to satisfy the interests of the residents and consequently made major changes to its proposed plans. It scrapped the option to build the large surface parking lot and instead opted for an underground parking lot. Listening to a specific call-out from the residents' community, the company also added designs that include a gray mesh-like feature and glass on its outside. So, this store would be unique. It would be the only IKEA store in the country to have colors other than its iconic blue and yellow colors. In addition, IKEA committed to investing $420,000 for a significant artistic feature that Mayor David Haubert said would add a "wow" factor to the site. IKEA preferred to partner with the city and the community to arrive at a solution that works for all. Any city would be happy to have a partner like IKEA.

A significant statement was made by Angele Robinson-Gaylord, President of U.S. Property at IKEA that highlights the management's focus on mutual benefit: *"It's been a long road, but the work we've done together has created a stronger blueprint for a retail property that serves the needs of the community and represents the kind of development of which we can all be proud."*

In a discussion with a friend, I asked him how the kids are doing at school. He had twins of the age of eleven. He said that they had been doing very well in the last three months and that he had taken more interest in their school activities. Out of curiosity, I asked what he did differently. He said he made a deal with them. He gave them the option that if they completed their homework within a specific time, then they would get their Wi-Fi time. He said that kids also understand that Wi-Fi is a necessity but understood that their father was doing this for their own good. Clearly, he knew their interests and they knew his. The deal was a win-win!

Now, let's follow a story about a seven-year old girl, Adia. According to her father at a family gathering, she had recorded an interesting video. Upon hearing about the video, people at the party now wanted to watch it. Remember we talked about positions earlier? Watching the video was their position. But Adia did not want everybody else to watch the video, and so she kept insisting that her father could not play the video. That was *her* position.

The father tried to convince her to share the video with friends at the party, saying it was a good video. However, Adia was stubborn and refused to agree with her father. Their discussion went on for some time. Eventually, her father gave up, but people wanted to watch the video to find what was interesting. At this point, the negotiation started in earnest. Everybody tried different things to get Adia to agree. One girl, Sarah, who was very eager to watch the video, persisted in negotiating with Adia. She tried several different strategies to convince Adia. First, she asked if Adia wanted some chocolate. Adia wanted chocolate but she still didn't want people to watch the video so that offer was ruled out. Next, Sarah knew that Adia liked lipstick a lot so she offered Adia a glowing lip balm. Adia was indeed tempted with the lip balm and agreed that she wanted lip balm, but insisted she didn't want the video to be played and that offer didn't help.

In this case, the interests of the people in the party were to watch this interesting video and have some fun but at the same time applaud Adia for it. On the other hand, Adia stated her interest to her father mentioning that she's shy, and that she feels that people will make fun of her after watching the video. So, how did the story end? Do you think Adia agreed and the friends got a chance to watch the video? We will get back to this story later on in the book when you will find out what happened. Until then, let's continue with the Prepare phase.

Know your Alternatives

We have covered some important topics, including the WHAM strategy and listing down interests so far in the Prepare phase of a negotiation. Let's introduce a couple of new concepts. This section is about knowing your *Base Level* and *Alternatives*.

Base Level

In a negotiation that involves a quantity (such as number of items) or any value (such as money, price, fees, or others), the concept of "*base level*" comes into effect. Base level is a decision point such as the lowest or highest quantity or value that you will accept. So, if you do not get your base level in the negotiation, you will not make a deal. You will walk away and not make a bad decision. If you are negotiating with a friend where you help him/her with homework in exchange for two bars of Kit Kat, your base level is two bars of Kit Kat. For anything less than that, you will not allow yourself to make a deal.

How important is the base level? It is vital to note the base level while preparing for the negotiation. It is a checkpoint and is useful to be aware of, but a good negotiation means to get better than the base level deal. In the example above, if you negotiated for three or more bars of Kit Kat, that would be a good deal.

Let's go back to Rahul's story and assume the base level for him would be to get a Disney+ subscription for three months. If he gets anything less than that, for example a Disney+ for 1 month, he might not want to make that deal and should be prepared to walk away or consider his alternatives.

Alternatives

While the base level could help you make or break a deal, there are situations when you might want to understand your "Plan B", also called *alternatives*. Strong alternatives provide confidence that even if you don't get a deal, you know that you could rely on the alternative.

You may wonder how one finds an alternative. Consider finding possible backup options in the following ways to determine the best alternative:

1)   Listing all the possible alternatives even if they seem small, because it might be possible to combine a couple of options to form a significant alternative;

2)   Ranking the alternative from best to worst, using factors like easy to get, better value, effectiveness, meeting the other person's interests; and

3)   Selecting the most effective alternative.

The alternative that is ranked the highest based on the factors above would be the most likely alternative to fall back on if the negotiation is not successful. This highest ranking, most effective alternative can be referred to as the **TRAIN (Top Ranked Alternative in Negotiation)**.

So, let's assume you are negotiating with your friends to play basketball on Saturday afternoon. If the negotiation does not go forward as planned, what are your alternatives? Your alternatives could be:

- Watching a movie;
- Taking an online class; or
- Video conferencing with friends.

In Rahul's case, there were five items in his list. Those were his initial options that he shared with his parents. But knowing that those options might not work (and keeping in mind that he will get a gift for his birthday for sure), he would also need to think about what would be the backup alternatives if he did not get any one of his listed items. These alternatives could include the following:

1. List any additional items which he might think could work for sure, such as books or board games;
2. Prepare a lighter version of his originally listed options, for example, reducing the Disney+ subscription to three months as an alternative or combining a couple of alternatives such as a Disney+ subscription for three months and a board game;
3. Consider a gift card for his favorite store such as Amazon or Lego; and
4. Bank on getting something similar to what his older brother got for his birthday.

After listing these alternatives, Rahul would need to rank these in order from best to the least, using factors such as which one would meet the parent's interests, what he likes most, what he is likely to get, etc. The best alternative is, in other words, his TRAIN. If his original list of options don't work, he can mention his TRAIN to his parents since he is guaranteed to get something for his birthday.

Along with the important action of finding your own alternatives, another vital action is to find out the other person's alternatives. At the time of preparing, all the available information can be used to analyze what could be their alternatives. In the case of Rahul, he would do well to determine what his parent's alternatives might be if his list is not accepted.

How likely you will be able to understand the other party's alternatives depends on how well you know them, their interests, and the circumstances of negotiation.

In the Engage phase, we will elaborate on how to build on the other person's alternatives, which in turn, may affect our own alternatives.

Assess types of negotiations

So far, in this chapter, we have reviewed the WHAM strategy, interests and alternatives in a negotiation. We will conclude the Prepare phase by understanding the types of negotiation. The results in a negotiation can differ based on the specific type of negotiation, and it is important to plan accordingly.

In this age of advanced technology, negotiations can happen face-to-face or remotely. The use of technology is rapidly increasing by the day, and everyone will have to adapt to new means of negotiation. Use of video technology is similar to having face-to-face negotiations with somebody in another location. Remote negotiations happen on the phone, email or online.

Let's review the various types of negotiation. All types of negotiations mentioned below could be carried out face-to-face or remote.

Two-party Negotiation
This is the most common type of negotiation that we all encounter on a daily basis which involves two parties negotiating to meet their objectives. The parties may be two individuals (such as a daughter and father) or two groups of people (such as two kids and their parents). The duration of these negotiations also varies. Sometimes these negotiations last for just a few minutes while other types can last for days or months.

When a two-party negotiation takes between two groups, proper understanding within the group members is vital. Proper understanding of interests and styles of all the group members becomes crucial. If, for example, two kids are negotiating with their parents to go to Disneyland, the two kids should first prepare and align between them.

Let's look at an example of a two-party negotiation between a father and son. The son expressed his interest to have a phone in 8th grade, and at this point, the negotiation started. The father had an interest to build responsibility in his son. He told him that having a phone requires discipline and responsibility, so the son would need to demonstrate maturity and responsibility by planning and preparing for the SAT Math and achieving a high score of 740+. The son got his phone when he cracked a high score in the SAT. This is a classical two-party negotiation. Both parties had expressed their interests, and achieving one's own interest was possible by helping the other person achieve his interest.

Multi-party Negotiation

Imagine a negotiation where you are negotiating to choose the place for your birthday party, and possibly having to negotiate with your parents as well as your best friends. You want to be able to meet the interests of your parents, friends, and yourself. Would you be able to negotiate to decide the ideal location to have your birthday party?

As the name suggests, these negotiations involve multiple parties and the objectives of all the parties come into play. Again, these parties may be multiple individuals or multiple groups. Such types of negotiations most frequently follow the joint-interests method. As the interests of multiple parties are involved, solutions need to address those objectives. So, this type of negotiation is generally much more difficult.

Similar to the two-party negotiation, if the multi-party negotiation is between or among groups, it is crucial to have agreement among the people within the group before negotiating with the other group. Thus, a proper understanding of interests and styles of all the group members becomes crucial. We will talk about styles in the next chapter.

Mediation

Mediation is another common way to conduct a negotiation. It is frequently used to settle or to compromise disputes or differences of opinion. Remember the story of the two sisters and orange that we discussed earlier in the story? The mother played the role of a *mediator*. A mediator helps to resolve the differences between two parties, and plays a very important role in the negotiation. In the case of mediation, the parties are able to reach a compromise since the mediator seeks a fair and positive outcome for both parties. If you are in a negotiation where it seems difficult to move forward or get a decision, seek a mediator's help. Avoid hostility or fighting, as that might not help at all.

A typical case of mediation in daily life is illustrated in the following story. During a family drive, a mother mentions that a friend was getting a fish tank. Within a few minutes, the twelve-year-old daughter started crying at the back seat in the car. Wondering what suddenly happened to their daughter, the parents asked her why she was crying, but she was reluctant to say anything. They assumed it was because of the videos she was watching on her phone, so they instructed her to stop watching. At this point, the daughter revealed she was crying because she felt that she would never get a pet.

Concerned about the incident, the father asked his daughter the next day, "Why did you start crying yesterday?" He wanted to ensure that she was able to articulate the concerns so that they could be addressed adequately.

She said, "Whenever I ask for a pet, mom says 'No.' Now I think that I will never be able to get a pet."

At this point, the father asked, "Have you ever thought why Mom refuses to get you a pet? Do you know how much work there is in caring for a pet!"

"I can do all the work and take care of the pet," the daughter said confidently. At this comment, the father explained: "If you want to convince Mom, you will need to show that you are responsible for the next three months by attending to all your daily activities quickly and helping with household chores. If you could do that, Mom could think about getting a pet." At the same time, they discussed what kind of pet the daughter would like to have and agreed that a small pet such as a hamster might be easier to take care of and most likely, would make her responsible.

Separately, the father spoke to his wife separately about the matter, expressing his concern that it was not good for the daughter to get so emotional about having a pet. He explained that the daughter was getting more responsible and was willing to help with more chores, so it might be time to get a small pet. This might help to keep the younger daughter engaged and responsible as well. The mother understood that a small pet is much less work and her interests were to keep the daughters happy. They agreed to get a pet in three months.

Coalition

A *coalition* refers to an alliance of multiple people or parties to join forces in a negotiation with another party. Multiple parties join a coalition because they have common objectives. Being in a coalition provides the strength of numbers to negotiate better. In many cases, multiple smaller or weaker parties join together to negotiate against a stronger party. Imagine when two or three siblings, who have the same objectives, join together to negotiate with one of the parents. This happens a lot at our home, and I am sure this happens with you too. The multiple parties in the coalition have to come together to discuss what are their interests for the negotiation in the Prepare phase as well as in the Engage phase. However, be aware that coalitions might become unstable because there are multiple parties in a coalition. Imagine you have a coalition of siblings and decide to negotiate about a certain topic but one of the siblings gives in before the objective is achieved. If you are in a coalition, properly understand what the objectives of the coalition are and work closely with the members.

A relevant story mentioned by an 8th grade student highlighted the coalition that occurs in their class at school. Often, the teacher gives an assignment to be completed in two days. The class comes together as a coalition to negotiate with her for an extension in the deadline. Has this happened to you? The coalition would need to work with the teacher in a creative way that helps to achieve her interest. In this case, the class stated that if they can get an extension of the date to turn in the assignment, they will cooperate (in the student's words "be nice") with the "sub" (substitute teacher) who is sitting in for the class teacher the next day. This sounded like an innovative solution and the teacher extended the deadline. (In this case, the class had some problems previously with the substitute teacher so this worked well for the teacher.)

Agent

In many situations, the parties choose not to (or are not permitted to), negotiate with each other directly. In these cases, they negotiate via an *agent*. An agent helps to negotiate on behalf of the person called the *principal*. The agent has to accomplish the objectives set forth by the principal.

Do you ever ask your sibling to help convince your parents to obtain something? Yes, that happens frequently. I have observed this myself. In this case, your sibling is your agent and you are the principal. The agent negotiates on your behalf with the parents.

It is important that the agent understands and works for the interests of the principal in the negotiation. The agent should not have a conflict of interest that could prevent them from making the best decision in the principal's favor. For example, you wanted your sibling's help to convince your parents about dining out. Now, the agent (sibling) might help you with that. But what if the agent has his/her preference of a cuisine? He/she might settle for a cuisine of his/her choice. In that case, the agent might not achieve the best interests of the principal (you). The value of an agent is the best when he/she helps to achieve an impactful negotiation keeping in mind all the interests of the principal.

Clearly, as you can see from the above example, the relationship between the principal and the agent needs to be strong so that they both understand the interests of each other. When interacting with the other party, the agent might have to make a quick decision. Here the agent must be aware of all the requirements of the principal. In this case, the siblings would be wise to agree prior to the negotiation with the parents, on what restaurant they want to dine in, whether they agree to take food to go, etc. This will help them plan for the negotiation to get the highest impact.

Click-Thru Negotiation
Last, but certainly not least, is a type of negotiations that has become very important in the last few years. I call this

"Click-Thru negotiation" as these negotiations are happening without any direct interactions between the parties. Rather, the negotiations are occurring online between a user on one side and the algorithm on the other side. In this type of negotiation, try all the different options and evaluate what the algorithm can offer. Sometimes, you might have to take a break (log out) and come back later to finalize.

How many of you have seen your parents shopping online? This is a common example of "click-thru" negotiation. Let's look at Amazon to understand this further. Amazon does not negotiate directly with users but instead has built the "click-thru" approach as a part of the overall shopping experience. Shoppers search for the item they intend to buy. The portal asks for their interests such as price range, choice between new or used items etc. and then generates multiple options. To add value, the shoppers are shown additional items that can be bundled with the item that the shopper is buying. Amazon provides the references in the form of ratings and reviews to further help in the customer's decision-making.

Amazon's subscription plan is another "click-thru" negotiation experience that seeks to offer some price benefits to get a commitment from the buyers. Amazon offers the option of buying some frequently bought items on a subscription plan at discounted prices rather than on a one-time purchase basis. Additional discounts are available for multiple items subscribed. The users can also pick a schedule for subscription or defer schedule with just a click of a button. Clearly, Amazon's algorithm is negotiating effectively with the user.

Summary of Prepare phase

The Prepare phase is your planning time to get you ready for the negotiation. In this phase, we discussed how to present your idea or item to the other person using WHAM Strategy. We then reviewed the importance of finding your interests and alternatives. We wrapped up by looking at the different types of negotiations for you to make your strategy.

• • •

PHASE 2: ENGAGE

You have prepared well in the initial phase of negotiation and have all the points covered that you want to discuss. You are now ready to take the next step: to engage with the other person. The Engage phase is where you get the results for all the planning and strategizing.

Steve Jobs once said, *"To me, ideas are worth nothing unless executed. They are just a multiplier. Execution is worth millions."* Negotiations will be effective if the preparation is executed well. In this section, we will learn how to engage effectively with the other person or persons.

In the Engage phase, all your efforts of preparation are put to practice in the actual interaction with the other person or persons. Note that you can prepare properly with full details, but if you cannot interact with the other person to pass on the message clearly, the negotiation will not move forward. In many cases, the Engage phase is far more critical than the preparation.

Some of the key considerations in the interaction are below.

Build on Interests

Remember that in the Prepare phase we discussed that it is important to list your interests? In the Engage phase, you have an opportunity to build further on the interests. So, in our discussions with the other person we can further add to our knowledge of the other person's interests. There are a few ways to do this:

- Talk to the other person(s) about their priorities;
- Confirm that your understanding of their interests still matches their priorities; and
- Help to satisfy their interests by listening carefully and discussing openly.

A vital step in building on the interests of the other party is to understand the objectives of the key decision-maker (the main person who makes the decision) so that you can help achieve their objectives. This is specifically important in some cultures where the decisions are made and influenced by one individual or a group of key individuals. Back to Rahul's example, if one of the parents is the key decision-maker, it is useful to understand what that parent wants.

Confirm Alternatives

After building on the interests, it is time to confirm alternatives. In the Prepare phase, we discussed our alternatives and TRAIN. From all the available information, we also tried to figure out the other party's alternatives.

In the Engage phase, by talking to the other party, you can confirm your alternatives and revise your TRAIN. Further, new information could confirm or change your understanding of the other party's alternatives. It is not always possible to understand or get the other person to mention his/her alternative. So, keep that in mind.

In Rahul's case, he would need to change his alternatives and try to understand his parents' alternatives during the discussion. His parents might not agree to any of the items he has mentioned in the negotiation. "Then what are they thinking about?" He can try to find out from his interaction.

Conduct

Finally, let's talk about special attributes that are vital in a negotiation. In the next chapter, we will discuss in detail the behaviors such as gaining trust and credibility, effective communication, and the focus on emotions and body language that impact negotiations. The conduct during the Engage phase needs focus on the below attributes:

- Courage

  An important consideration as part of the communication is to have the courage to ask. In many cases, we hold back our views due to the fear of asking for too much. While the mind considers something excessive and fears that we will be declined, the chances are that we will miss out on getting something because we did not muster enough courage to speak out.

- Persistence

  The other aspect to consider as part of the engagement is Persistence. People question if this behavior is effective. Some people might view this persistence as an inconvenience but it can be helpful in many cases. In my opinion, it is a significant part of negotiations. Persistence is the ability to push on towards achieving an objective through continuous engagement and communication. Even if the result derived from persisting is not exactly as originally intended, you can at least get a result, which is better than having no result. Have you ever heard the other person saying, "It's not negotiable?" Well, there is always scope for negotiation. You do not need to stop at "No" as the answer. All you need to know is how to build the story around the negotiation.

  Kids, in general, are great at showing this behavior when they negotiate as they are determined not to give up. One such example was a story narrated by a friend recently. A 10-year-old once came to his dad and said, "Dad, I always have to come to you and trouble you for the password for downloading any game on my iPad. Also since you are traveling and you are busy, I cannot reach you and do not want to disturb you. So why don't you give me your password and I will let you know when I am downloading the game". A smart technique used by a little kid. He highlighted the interests of the dad and offered to inform after downloading the game. In this case, the dad almost fell for the strategy but in time realized what just hit him and declined. This did not deter the 10-year-old and he persisted by trying different ways every few weeks.

It was amusing to observe a toddler about a year old on one of my flights. I believe the toddler wanted to walk around the airplane. However, the mother did not want to let him walk around. The toddler would wail for a while and then stop to look at his mom. And if he did not get an anticipated response, he would start wailing again. One can never say what was going on in his mind but if these were negotiation tactics, I believe over a time he would become an effective negotiator.

- Spontaneity
  An important skill to help in negotiations is spontaneity. This term means to think quickly. It helps with quick decision-making and reacting according to circumstances and developments in a negotiation

discussion. Proper preparation and practice will help during the actual engagement with the other party.

- Negoptimism
  Well, is this a word? I have created this word. It means a positive attitude that is required in any negotiation interactions since it produces better results. Don't allow biased thinking to affect your views before even trying to negotiate. I have often heard my kids say, "No, Mommy is not going to agree!" My question to them is, "How do you even know without asking?" With proper preparation and engagement, you can make the other person agree. You have to believe in this!

Presenting your point

Do you know that any discussion is effective if the other party gets a positive feeling? Thus, it is important to be able to frame a conversation or a proposal so that it appears as a benefit and makes the other party feel happy.

Note that this also applies to negotiations. In a negotiation, it is useful to present a point as a benefit to the other party, that is, something good that will generate better results and get a positive reaction from the other party. They are likely to be more welcoming of your proposals and work with you on options. Bring out the good points about what you are proposing in order to create a positive feeling. Similarly, sometimes it is useful to highlight any negative outcomes if the other party does not follow your point. This will mean that it is good for them to do what you are presenting. This leads them to believe in the positive aspects of your proposal.

A friend shared an example that illustrates the benefits of presenting positively in a negotiation. His daughter always starts the discussion with her parents by highlighting the good things she has done during the day. She also mentions that she will finish her homework but asks if she can play a game online after. This is important because by stating the benefit that the parents see first, they are more likely to agree for her to play the game.

On the other hand, if the other person sees any risk in the negotiation discussions, they will go on the back foot and feel reluctant to develop trust. In this case, they will be unlikely to make any decisions or create solutions, and will block off the options provided to them. Hence, any information presented to the other person needs to ensure that it brings out the positive.

Here's a real life example that you all have likely experienced:

Child - "Mommy, please can I use your phone?"

Mommy - "No!"

Child - "Please, for 10 minutes?"

Mommy - "No!"

Child - "But I need to send my teacher a video of my dance that she requested."

So, what would the child have done differently? Starting the discussion by asking for the phone created a barrier in the mother's mind. If the child had started the conversation with something more positive or explained first that she got a request from her teacher to send a video, it would have been a different conversation and a different result!

Child - "My teacher asked me to send her a video of my dance. She will be using it to check how well I am dancing now."

Mommy - "OK! Go ahead!"

Child - "Mommy, please can I use your phone?"

Mommy - "Sure."

Child - "Thanks, Mommy!"

Do you see the difference?

In Rahul's story, to convince the parents for a Disney+ subscription for one year, he would have to promise them something that he thinks would work for both himself and his parents. He could propose that he would only watch for a few hours a week since it would help him relax after he completed his homework. Only when it is a promise that sounds favorable to the parents can he get a quick decision in his favor. These kinds of negotiations and situations are very common in day-to-day life and especially for you, my young readers.

A daughter was negotiating with her parents to allow her to download an app called V-Live on her phone. She prepared a note to share with her parents. This is what the note said:

"What is V-live?

V-live is an app where K-pop idols can create videos and upload them to the app. Fans can then comment on the video (like YouTube) and K-pop stars can reply.

Pros:

- *I can watch videos about my favorite idols.*
- *I don't need to upload any pictures (like Instagram). That means no one will see my face. The only thing one can do is post comments.*

- *I don't think you would let me comment yet, but the only reason I want V-live is to follow what idols are doing.*
- *This way, no one will know who I am, but I could see everything on the app."*

Analyzing this a bit further, we see a positive method of presenting her point. She clearly highlighted how this is important and positive to the parents and their interests (namely privacy), in addition to stating her interests.

"High value–low value" strategy

Here's an interesting strategy of presenting something that immediately gets a reaction from the other person. It is a strategy most people know and use, but I will highlight it for you. There are two ways to use this strategy:

1. First, the strategy presents two things one after the other, and the first thing has a high value and the second has a low value, which leads to a decision toward buying or getting the second thing. Often, sales strategy presents a high value item first and then a lower value item immediately after, to sell the lower value item.
2. Secondly, this strategy is also used cleverly to present a few items together, some of high value and some of

lower value. As compared to the higher value item, the lower value item seems much better. Hence, people accept the item with the smaller value. Bear in mind that the goal is to sell more of the smaller value items. This strategy could also be applied to present something with a higher adverse impact and immediately show something with a lower impact, so that a decision is made for the lower impact item.

A story from my family highlights this concept well. My daughter asked for tickets to a music concert. She introduced the high value by saying, "You know for the upcoming concert my friends bought tickets for $300." After introducing the high value, she said, "Since we agreed to also buy the tickets, I did some research and found tickets for just $70." The decision was easy for the parents.

Another example that a friend highlighted was that his eight-year-old son started by asking for something big like a $150 Lego set. When the parents refused, he made a long face and said, "But it's been so long since I got a Lego. Can I at least have this one? It's only $20!" So, he uses the high value-low value strategy to make the second item appear a better option to negotiate with the parents.

Remember I mentioned earlier that the "high value-low value" strategy applies in Rahul's case. Rahul presented five items in his list to his parents. Of the five items, three were of high value or were more complex. Based on this strategy, the parents would immediately remove those options. So, that left two options to choose from, and these were the options of Rahul's interest.

Anchoring

In the case of a negotiation which involves a number (for example, a price or quantity), the starting position used by either of the persons in the negotiation is called the *anchor*. The anchor then determines how the other person will react for the rest of the negotiation. Do you know that virtually everyone very commonly uses an anchor, almost every day? Have you ever been in (or heard) a conversation like the one below? Let's look at an anchor in a typical conversation:

A mother says to her child, "You will only get 30 minutes of TV time!" This is the mother's anchor for how much TV time she will grant the child.

The child's response to this is, "Please, can I get 60 minutes?" This is the child's anchor.

Both the mother and child expect that the final result, after one or more rounds of going back and forth, will be close to their respective anchors. The anchors drive the discussion towards the level that each party wants to achieve.

When and how do you find your anchor?

Anchors need to be determined during the Prepare phase, and you should be able to support your position by strong reasons such as the available facts and circumstances, proper research, previous examples, etc. It is important for the anchors to be justifiable. The other person might ask you for the reasons of the anchor, and if you cannot provide them, it can cause loss of trust.

In the earlier example about TV time, the mother could have justifiable criteria such as TV time that was already granted earlier in the day, time to go to bed, etc., and the child could have justifiable criteria such as two hours of studies completed, extra chores completed, watching one hour-long episode of your favorite show, etc. However, if the child asks for two hours of TV without giving a strong reason, the mom might not be convinced.

Also, beware of some tactics people use called *lowball* or *highball* to divert attention. Lowball refers to an anchor that is significantly lower than expected (for example a buyer who offers to pay a very low price) and Highball refers to a significantly high anchor (for example a seller might ask for a high price). In our example, if you ask for two hours of TV, it might be a highball, and if the parent gives you only 15 minutes, it might be a lowball.

Further, while you prepare a good anchor during the Prepare phase, the Engage phase is vital for you to mention the anchor to the other person. You can also make adjustments to your anchors in this phase as you learn more about the other party's anchors. Note that anchors are a starting point for the conversation but are not the end of the negotiation.

Who should make the first offer of the anchor?

One of the common questions about anchors is who should start with their anchor. If both persons in a negotiation have justifiable reasons for their anchors, it doesn't matter who makes the first offer, as both will present strong reasons for their anchors.

Anchor and Alternatives
Remember we discussed alternatives/TRAIN previously under the Prepare phase? Anchor has close correlation with alternatives. If person A has strong alternatives/TRAIN, any starting anchors from person B would not scare person A. The strong TRAIN might also enable person A to have the

courage to put in the first offer. However, if the alternatives/TRAIN for person A are weak, he/she would be more likely to accept person B's anchor.

Summary of Engage Phase

To sum up, the Engage phase is the "make or break" phase since the negotiation is dependent on the successful engagement with the other person or persons. We discussed the importance of presenting your point and the significance of anchors.

• • •

PHASE 3: CLOSE

After all the hard work in the Prepare and Engage phases, it is crucial that the negotiation is finalized and closed well. In the Close phase, we will look at three primary steps to close the negotiation successfully. Let's review.

Agreement

This is a very important step, my young negotiators. In some negotiations, multiple issues and solutions are discussed. The parties then agree on a bundle of solutions in this step of the Close phase, and ensure that all agreed points are well understood and final. If anybody else needs to be included to get the agreement, it should be done at this stage to bring the negotiation to a completion.

It is vital to know upfront who the decision- maker(s) is (are) who need(s) to provide their okay to the points discussed. This is valuable in a situation where you might have concluded negotiations with a person who could be overruled by other decision-makers on their side. Do you think that an agreement with your dad needs to be approved by your mom too or vice versa?

In some cases, this might even be used as a tactic by some people to get an advantage. As an example, you may go through the whole negotiation with the other person(s), and then near the end of the discussion they introduce another person who needs to agree. This last minute condition might throw off the negotiation, and lead you to make a quick, rushed decision. Therefore, it is important to know upfront who all have to agree and approve.

Record

In many negotiations, after the agreement or consensus is obtained on all the terms and solutions, the next step is to ensure that all agreed terms are properly recorded via a written document or email. This ensures that there is no misunderstanding or disagreement after the negotiation is complete. Of course, in most of your negotiations with your parents, siblings or friends, you would not record terms or decisions. However, in other cases such as a negotiation with the teacher, you might need to send a text message or an email to list the terms and final decisions.

Handshake

"So is it a deal?" You have probably heard your mom or dad ask this question. This is a way to say that the negotiation is complete and you can seal the deal with a handshake. After the agreement and recording, the final step is the handshake that leads to a closing of the negotiation. In many cases, handshake refers to signing the contract to close the deal.

Do you remember Rahul's story? In his letter to his parents, he provided some space at the bottom for his parents to write their choice of his birthday gift and sign. This was his way to record and finalize the decision.

Summary of Close phase

The negotiation is not complete until it is properly closed. I heard the phrase "Nothing is agreed until everything is agreed!" at a Harvard negotiation seminar and it stuck with me. After all, if you have put all the effort to come to this closing stage, you will want to get the benefits of the efforts. In this phase, we looked at the steps to close the negotiation.

• • •

Chapter Summary

We have reached the end of this crucial chapter that presented the science of negotiation. Here we discussed the aspects that laid the foundation for a successful negotiation. We discussed the important phases - Prepare, Engage and Close - to be able to put the best foot forward in the negotiation.

Now you should be able to answer the questions below.

What do I need to do to prepare for the negotiation?

Remember to prepare your WHAM Strategy, list down your interests and assess the other person's interests, know your alternatives, and assess the type of negotiations.

What do I need to do while engaging with the other person?

Focus on the confirming interests and alternatives, conduct, learn about presenting your point, and know about anchors.

What are the necessary steps to close the negotiation?

Come to an agreement with the other person, record the agreement either by writing or verbally, and finalize with a handshake.

CHAPTER 4

THE ART OF NEGOTIATION

Concepts and terms explained in this chapter

BEHAVIORS THAT MATTER

Key aspects - Trust and credibility, Communication essentials, and Emotions and body language

Styles - Understanding how styles impact negotiation

POWER OF INFLUENCING

Connecting:
- Reciprocation: Give and take
- Bonding: Strong relationships
- References: Recommendations or reference

Committing:
- Promise: Fulfilling a commitment
- Vested: Alignment with others

Controlling:
- Authority: A leverage or power
- Loss Anxiety: Feeling of loss
- Vividness: Extraordinary way to present

Okay, my friends, let's move forward in your learning journey toward becoming a better negotiator.

In the previous chapter, we looked at the science of negotiation with the three phases that form the crux of the negotiation process. In this chapter, I will introduce the art of negotiation, which explains the behaviors that matter and the power of influencing or persuading that plays a major role in negotiations.

. . .

BEHAVIORS THAT MATTER

What I present here are standard behaviors we all know about. However, it is critical to look at how these behaviors need to be applied while engaging in the negotiation process. Negotiating is about bringing the right attitude to the table. The behaviors are vital and can make or break a negotiation. Appropriate behaviors are necessary in all types of negotiations.

We will first discuss key aspects of behaviors in general. In the latter part of this Chapter, we will discuss people's styles that are essential components of behaviors demonstrated during negotiations.

I have categorized the key aspects into three major buckets: Trust and credibility, Communication, and Emotions and Body Language.

1. Trust and credibility

As with anything in life, it is vital to build trust and credibility, and negotiations are no different. Don't you expect behavior from others that makes us trust them? If yes, then it is logical that when you are negotiating, specific attention needs to be placed on your appropriate behaviors to build trust. Actions that will help you build trust and credibility are explained below:

- Earn respect: Trust comes from being respected, and respect comes from not only saying the right things but also demonstrating that you understand the other party and would like to collaborate with them.

- Be Fair: Trust can be earned by demonstrating integrity and fairness. Fairness is an important component in the process of negotiation and paying specific attention to what all parties need will help in developing trust. If you are not fair, somebody will call it out. If you agree that you will do something, stick to the promise. If you don't, you will be deemed unfair and lose respect. When one girl was being unfair, her mother called out to her, "It's very unlikely of you to be unfair."

- Be Flexible: Being flexible helps to demonstrate partnership, and is necessary in long-term relationships.

- Compromise (as required): In many cases, people might be close to finalizing the negotiation even when the decision is not fully in their favor. Being open to a compromise in these situations helps so that efforts, time, cost etc. to reach that stage are not wasted. However, a compromise should not become a substitute or excuse for not putting in the best effort in negotiations. Compromise might help you go past the finish line!

2. Communication

Communication is another factor that plays a critical role in all our interactions and is of utmost significance in all negotiations. It is well understood that without proper communication, there is no chance of success in negotiation. I cannot emphasize enough how valuable good communication can be for your interactions, and in building the necessary relationships.

The best time to build effective communication is right at the start of the engagement with the person sitting across the table. Begin with greetings or positive messages to build connections with the other person. A softer tone at the beginning will open up the communication channel. In some cases, if it becomes difficult to communicate with the other party directly, mediators will need to do the communication.

The key to effective communication is also to find the right communication lines. Most times, you have to decide with whom to communicate in order to move a negotiation forward. Isn't that right? For example you might have to decide whether to communicate with your mother or father.

Several aspects need attention to ensure that you communicate properly:

- First, proper communication starts with being a good listener. Have you ever had a situation where somebody is talking to you and you also start to talk? You need to wait and listen to them with your full attention, otherwise you will not know what they have said.

  Listening has two clear benefits: Firstly, the other person feels better that you were considerate enough to listen before speaking, and secondly, they would be able to express their views freely making them open-minded. Further, listening produces more information on their needs, and allows you to effectively convey your points in the negotiation.

- In order to get the most information from the other person, the best approach is to ask open-ended questions that are meant to get proper and full responses from the other person. Don't ask closed-ended questions that can be answered by a "yes" or "no" answer because then you don't really get much detail of their view to help you to find solutions for a successful negotiation.

- A crucial part of communication is to clearly express the benefits that the other party will derive from the negotiation. In common professional terms, it is known as WIIFM (stands for "What's In It For Me") and is important to gain trust of the other party.

- Regularly ask for clarification and elaboration, and request relevant examples. Repeat and rephrase what the other party says to confirm understanding. Acknowledgement ensures that you understand the interests of the other party and prevents any differences in understanding. Clarification is particularly necessary when you communicate with someone (for example, a friend or classmate) from another culture who speaks a different language. Special attention is needed in communication with them.

Sometimes, when communication with words does not work, it is OK to use props such as a drawing or pictures to explain the point better. For example, a mom and daughter entered a hair salon for the daughter's haircut. The mother mentioned that she wanted her daughter to get a short haircut. The daughter said she just wanted to trim and texture her hair. They negotiated for a little while. As they kept arguing, I realized that there were differences. However, it quickly turned into assessing their interests. The mother and daughter started looking at online hairstyle pictures. The daughter explained what she wanted and the mother explained why it did not work. Soon they agreed on one style that seemed to satisfy both their interests. It helped to sit down and discuss (with pictures) what each wanted and come to a mutually acceptable conclusion.

3. Emotions and Body Language

Finally, emotions and body language play a big part in behaviors. You all know what Intelligence Quotient (IQ) is. It is a measure of intelligence. Emotional Intelligence or Emotional Quotient (EQ) is another crucial aspect of all interactions. It is a measure of how you deal with emotions, your own and those of the other party. Often people consider IQ having an upper hand while I think EQ is just as important. Both are not adequate just by themselves.

- Focus on body language. Your body language is vital in conversations. You can also learn from observing others' body language. Your own approach can be adjusted according to the body language demonstrated by the other party.

- Confidence. Another primary behavior is to beam with confidence. The confidence arising from body language drives a point home. Confidence also leads you to be calm and composed. However, there is a fine line between being confident or appearing overconfident.

- Be empathetic. The feel-good factor that is essential in finalizing a deal comes from being considerate to the other party's feelings and making things work. This contributes positively to building trust. Ever wondered why kids say, "Please, pretty please!"? It wins the empathy from the other person. Empathy also works differently for different people. For some kids and adults, it is important to show them more politeness and empathy. So if you know any such people, show more empathy.

- Control emotions. Effectively managing your own emotions is critical. At the same time, while it is necessary to be considerate to the other party's feelings, don't be shy to subtly call out their angry emotions to drive the discussions to a smooth conclusion. Along this line of thought, it is key to avoid hostility that can break up any communications. Showing anger only generates more anger. How many times have you been angry and it causes one of the parents to be angry? Anger always spoils the way.

Further, as you grow older and start dealing with many people at school and college, you will deal with people of diverse cultures who behave differently. In addition to the above behaviors, negotiating across cultures is an important skill in today's global environment. For example, I observed my Indian friend's kids (aged 14 and 9) discussing with their Chinese friends (aged 15 and 11) who were visiting to celebrate an Indian festival. The kids were negotiating on what to eat for a snack. On a festive occasion such as this, Indian families do not eat non-vegetarian food. It was interesting that the Chinese kids knew this. And the older kid had the courtesy to ask, "But I think we should not eat any snacks with eggs today, right?" This demonstrated good awareness of culture, and the ability to understand, respect, and adopt, as much as possible, the cultural values that apply to the other party.

Keep the behaviors mentioned below in mind for the future when dealing with people from different cultures.

- Impressions: Imagine you are doing a school project and have to negotiate with a faculty to join the band class. In this case, it is a formal setting. Would it be appropriate to show up in a jersey and shorts? Similarly, the manner in which you meet and greet a person is very different across cultures. The well-known adage "A first impression is a lasting impression" means to try your best to create a good impression. This will play a big role in how your negotiation discussions will progress. After the first meeting, you may decide how you want to behave in future meetings based on the experience with the person.

- Body contact and body language: Along the same lines as impressions is touch, contact and body language. Understanding and respecting other cultures helps to avoid behaviors that could harm reputation. Sign language also needs proper attention.

- Punctuality: Focus on time considerations differ by culture. In some cultures, following the time commitments is a strict requirement while in other cultures there is no emphasis on punctual behavior.

- Other considerations: There are several other criteria that differ by culture, including gift-giving, level of assertiveness, and the extent of being pushy or nagging. Specific awareness of these criteria based on the other party's culture are beneficial to the overall success of the negotiations.

Styles

The behaviors are supported by understanding of your own style as well as that of the other person. As mentioned in Chapter 2, individual styles matter in how people conduct and behave in a negotiation.

Negotiating style differs from individual to individual, and therefore attending to the differences in styles becomes critical. If not adequately considered and/or managed during the negotiation discussions, these differences can result in adverse reactions and behaviors.

In this section, I will explain the different styles so that you will better understand your own style as well as the style of the decision-maker on the other side. That said, remember that in some cases you will need to change or adjust your style and actions according to the other person's style.

There are five key types of styles. Let's review these styles to see how they differ and how they impact negotiations.

1)   Collaborating or "It's a win-win" style

A person with this style likes to work collaboratively with other people in a negotiation. Solutions are derived based on partnership and agreement to achieve mutual gains.

Specifically, this style calls for:

- Focusing on both parties' interests;
- Nurturing a long term partnership; and
- Building trust by achieving joint benefits.

Most commonly, people with this style ask questions to understand the other party's interests in order to be able to provide options that benefit all. What's more, this style results in creativity. The collaboration and focus on "win-win" brings out the best in these individuals.

I observed an interesting example of the Collaborating style that I would like to share with you. Two girls, ten-year-old Nadia and six-year-old Ayesha, were sitting in the back seat of a car. At a stop, Ayesha walked out of the car and Nadia sat with her legs on top of the two seats (hers and Ayesha's) comfortably reading a book. When Ayesha returned, she wanted to sit. At this moment, Nadia came up with an idea. She told Ayesha to sit and put her legs on top of Nadia's legs that rested on the seat. Nadia's request meant that she would be able to sit with her legs on the seat and Ayesha would get a cushion under her legs. She asked Ayesha to try the seating arrangement once and if it didn't work, they could go back to the old way. Demonstrating the Collaborating style, Nadia came up with a different solution that could work for both of them. It turned out that Ayesha liked the seating arrangement and both were comfortable and happy.

As young readers and negotiators, I recommend you focus on this style. If your style is different, you should try to adopt this collaborative approach to the extent possible.

In the case of conflicts between parties, a person with this style spends time to discuss options that benefit all. They believe in creative problem-solving in a conflict situation.

2) Compromising or "Give and take" style

A person with this style focuses on meeting the other party's needs on some things (depending on the situations) but expects to get his/her points on other things. The idea is to give something valuable to the other party but get something back in exchange.

In many cases, the expected result is to reach a middle ground so that both parties feel that they got a satisfactory deal. Remember the story of the two sisters who were arguing over one orange? In the end, they had to settle for a compromise. Many people think of this style as a "win-win" because it results in getting a deal for both parties. However, as you saw in the story of the two sisters, the compromise was not the best solution for them since it did not create the jointly beneficial solutions that are generated by the Collaborating style.

People with this style:

- Seek to share with others something important to them while getting some back;
- Are willing to reach a middle ground; and
- Believe in reciprocation.

In general, most kids are the best examples of the Compromise style. Quite often, we have a scenario where the negotiation between a kid and a parent or between kids ends up in a compromise. A recent example from a friend illustrates this style. The boy was extraordinarily smart in mathematics. The parents recognized his skill and sent him to two math enrichment classes. He performed well but told friends in a discussion, "I am not interested in mathematics and attend only because my parents insist." The parents got to know this. In the fear of burning out the boy too quickly, the father came up with an idea. He said to his son, "You know all the math work and classes you do is good, but we need to make sure you do something of your interest. Would you like to do something else that you enjoy?" The son said, "Yeah! I would really like to go for basketball coaching!" After a bit of thought and planning, his father agreed to undertake the cost and effort for the son's request for basketball classes but on the condition that the son continued with the math classes and received a certain percentage score. A healthy compromise in this example demonstrates that the style works with kids. In this case, the father also adapted well to the Compromising style.

In the case of conflict situations, this style expects exchanging and sharing concessions. The idea is not to get the best but to reach a meaningful *middle ground*. As mentioned under the Collaborating style, this style might also need to adopt a different style in some cases. Furthermore, if the counterpart uses an aggressive tactic to take a bigger stake, a person with the Compromising style might be the one to give in.

3) Competing or "Prove my own point" style

Do you have a parent or friend who always reacts strongly and aggressively to any points in a negotiation? A person with this style is typically the Competing style whose primary objective is to prove a point and get people to agree with them.

For people with this style, the approach is to:

- Focus on their own interests;
- Be assertive right from the start; and
- Be open to using aggressive tactics to accomplish their objectives

Negotiation with a person of this style could prove challenging. Since they show aggression right from the start, it is necessary to be cognizant of their behavior and to match it in a very careful way. Don't be scared of the person with this style, and don't start to counter their emotions. If two people with this style engage in a negotiation, there is a high probability of failure in negotiation.

While sometimes being competitive might be okay, the Competing style could negatively affect the negotiation in most cases if the other party loses trust. A Competing style negotiator should try to adopt the Collaborating or

Compromising style in certain circumstances to be a successful negotiator.

A story narrated by a friend explains how a solution can be provided to people of the Competing style to make them collaborative or compromising. His son asked if they could buy a PlayStation (PS) as schools were closing for summer soon. The father, who demonstrates the Competing style, refused and said they cannot think of buying it for the next 4-5 months. Not getting a positive response from his father, the son went back to his room. After a while, he returned with a couple of gift cards and some cash, and told his father that he had saved some money that he can contribute toward the cost of the PS. He also suggested that they could sell the old Xbox. The father was amazed, and agreed to discuss further.

When a conflict arises, a Competing style negotiator expects to get the upper hand. In such cases, there are ways to effectively engage with the person. Arriving at and offering multiple options can be useful. Often, some options that might be important to a competing person might be possible to offer easily. A good analysis of these options and providing them as you go will help calm down a person with this style and start being more open to the discussion. Understandably, this might not be easy in conflict situations. However, where the likelihood of an agreement is not looking feasible, consider getting help, as was demonstrated in the story of the two sisters. In the age of kings and empires, competing styles would often result in wars. However, in today's age, conflicts could be resolved by a third person who acts as a mediator.

4) Accommodating or "Will do it for you" style

A person with this style is likely to be heavily influenced by what the other party needs and, therefore, runs the risk of giving in to their requests. The primary goal of these individuals is to grow and/or maintain relationships. Hence, they are likely to accommodate the other person's requests.

Characteristics of people with this style are:

- Possess higher EQ, in general, which focuses on relationships;
- Impacted by feelings such as trust and empathy; and
- May make unfavorable decisions for themselves to maintain relationships.

People with this style generally arrive at a discussion with the goal of managing relationships. Their accomplishment is in making it through the negotiation without hurting feelings and relationships. They also make concessions frequently. In my observations, some people in negotiations have announced concessions even before the other party has stated their position. People with this style are most likely to be taken advantage of people with other styles.

In case of conflicts with a person of an Accommodating style, it is beneficial to discuss relationships and build on the Emotional Quotient (EQ). Attention to emotions will help pave the way forward in negotiations.

5) Avoiding or "I lose but you also lose" style

Finally, people with Avoiding style stay away from any direct conversations that may seem to be unpredictable or challenging.

Primary characteristics of this style are to:

- Avoid confrontation or leave it to others to deal with;
- Procrastinate and delay tough decisions;
- Share their views via offline media (letters, notes, emails) or engage in direct "to the point" interaction if absolutely required

People with the Avoiding style tend to leave difficult conversations aside or defer those conversations to others. They prefer to work toward a decision quickly. There is no focus on discussing a variety of options. In many cases, people with this style simply walk away and abruptly end a discussion that does not support their views and interests. They do not collaborate to build solutions.

Remember that being adamant is also similar to an Avoiding style because your inflexibility demonstrates that you do not want to listen to the other person. This behavior does not help anybody and will likely result in a stalemate.

When you engage with people with this style, it is better to persist with them. Initiating discussions that drive towards building options and asking leading questions might help with getting a response.

In case of conflict, it is beneficial to give the persons with this style some time to think through everything. Engage them by discussing something they have shown as an interest.

Do you know anybody with this style? Many kids and young adults demonstrate this style. After working with them to address points that might be holding them back, they might switch to the Compromising style.

My daughter often demonstrates the Avoiding style. In certain situations, getting a desired response becomes extremely difficult. But there are options available in a negotiation, and it is good to wait for the right opportunity to steer the negotiation in the right direction.

She was part of the girls' cricket team in her previous school and developed a keen interest in the sport. A few months ago, after having taken a break from cricket, she started cricket coaching again. After coaching for a few months, her school's team manager at her middle school asked me if she would be interested in joining the school team. There was an upcoming inter-school cricket tournament in which any school could register if they had twelve players on a team. While it was beneficial to the team as they needed more players, it was a lucky break for my daughter as she had just started training a few months ago. I immediately understood the value of this opportunity for her and agreed to register her for the team.

Now commenced the negotiation with my daughter to play on the school cricket team. Though cricket was a keen interest for her, she was, nonetheless, apprehensive. She started practicing with the school team that consisted mostly of boys who played hard. She was not comfortable practicing with them due to their rough style of play. When I discussed with her about registering for the school team, she was adamant that she would not play with them. I told her that I had already committed to paying the registration fees, but she can choose whether to play or not. She was indifferent, however, and stood firm with her position. It was a difficult negotiation.

A few days passed by and I had registered her without her confirmation. I had already paid the registration fees, so I had no other alternative. However, I knew that persistence works well in these situations, so I realized I had to use a different approach to frame this discussion. My first objective was to get her to go on the field.

A couple of days before the first match, I got a much-needed opportunity to help deal with the Avoiding style. Indeed, a lucky break in a scenario that seemed like a lost cause. I read a message that the committee was looking for parent volunteers to help supervise the matches. This was my chance to try a different approach. I told her that I had volunteered to be the umpire (referee) in the match and that she could come just to watch the match. I knew she liked to watch cricket so she would most likely agree. And she did!

Step 1 was achieved in the negotiation to bring her to the field. At the game, she watched me on the field as the umpire and watched her team play the game. She realized that it was fun to play. At the end of the match, I told her that she just needed to be on the field to get comfortable. I eased her concerns by telling her that she would not need to bat or bowl, as her team was strong. So, she agreed to go and field. Step 2 was achieved as she was on the field for the next game. It was then a matter of time before she got more confidence to go out and bat or bowl. Building confidence by helping her feel comfortable was critical. I was successful in the negotiation to bring her to the field by understanding her interests and attending to her preferences. It was a win-win for both of us.

Rahul demonstrated the Avoiding style too by giving the parents a letter. In a negotiation, he would have to evaluate if he should adopt a different style, such as the Collaborating style, to get better results.

. . .

POWER OF INFLUENCING

In the process of negotiation, influencing the other party becomes key to achieving your desired outcomes. Have you ever:

- wondered how to get the full focus from the other party?
- thought how you could get a more favorable response or reception from the other party?
- wished that you could get some tips to influence somebody better?
- wondered why some people are so good at persuading others?

Answers to these questions lie in understanding and developing influencing skills. When applied correctly, influencing techniques are expected to generate a specific behavior and the response that you expect from the other party. Imagine the power you gain from these influencing skills for your negotiation.

In this section, we will study situations in which these techniques might work. In fact, we use them daily. Most times, we do not realize that we are using these techniques. Also, since others might be applying these techniques in discussions with you, it is important to understand the effect these are having on your negotiation. Do you know that most sales and marketing strategies that companies use one or more of these techniques? You have surely heard of the rush in the stores during Black Friday sales. That is one of the techniques. Though the techniques might not work in all situations, in some cases, more than one technique might be applied but one might have a greater impact than the others. At the end of this section, we will see an impressive use of multiple techniques in one situation.

The influencing techniques can be broken down into three categories: **Connecting, Committing and Controlling**. Each of these categories includes specific techniques. We will now review each of these techniques with examples and stories to explain how they can trigger expected behavior. It is important to note that the other party might also be good at using them in negotiations.

See below a picture of the three major categories and the techniques under each of those categories.

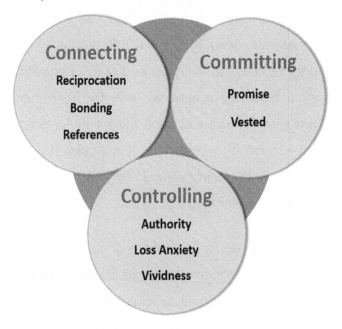

Image 3 - Influencing techniques by category

Connecting techniques

As the name suggests, these techniques are used to connect with the other party. The goal is to develop a relationship that can be leveraged in influencing during negotiation. In this category, there are three distinct ways to make the connection: **Reciprocation, Bonding and References**. Each of these techniques is important in its own right. However, they can even be combined in a negotiation. The effect of the techniques might vary based on the situation. Let's review in more detail.

Reciprocation

The common phrase "You scratch my back and I scratch yours" is an easy way to explain this technique. It is also commonly referred to as "give and take". Reciprocation is the human behavior where we feel the responsibility to return any kind of helpful actions, favors and generosity that we receive from another person. It is a powerful technique to be used in influencing others. Let's discuss how this is done and what benefits are gained.

Reciprocation occurs in case of the actions below:

1) Actions that occurred prior to a negotiation:
   These are reciprocal actions that have happened in the past and that can be called upon during the current negotiation. They act as a way to get another person to do something in return. In some cases, a prior action can be so significant that it generates multiple return actions in future. As we will see when we talk about the Bonding technique next, when reciprocation is repeated over and over, it converts into a long-term connection.

When I was younger, we used to receive *Reader's Digest* magazine mailers regularly, and the package would contain free stickers, calendars and other useful items. I did not understand the concept of reciprocation at that time, but I can now relate to the technique used by *Reader's Digest*. The idea was to provide these items to generate future reciprocal action to subscribe for the magazine.

2) Actions during the current negotiation:
The following actions occur during the current negotiation and help in deriving a reciprocal behavior:

- Providing items or gifts;
- Taking actions beneficial to the other party; and
- Providing accommodations or concessions.

We all know that reciprocation results from providing items or gifts. Similarly, taking some favorable actions such as being open and sharing information generates the anticipated behavior from the other party to share information.

Also, note that I mentioned "providing concession." Concession means to be flexible and relax your stand. As such, even concessions are actions that would derive reciprocation. For example, if your mom asked you to play a video game for 30 minutes. After you talked to her, she agreed to give you 45 minutes. Granting you an extra 15 minutes of playtime is a concession. Provide a concession and see the benefit when the other person also makes concessions.

Can you think of any other examples of reciprocation from your personal experiences?

Have you ever helped a friend with their homework without expecting anything in return but later they have helped you with something you need? This is an example of prior action that gets you a reciprocation.

When evaluating what influencing techniques can be applied to a negotiation, it is important to understand the power of reciprocation under different circumstances. Beware of a reciprocation action that is going to compel you to do something in exchange without your liking. This might be a tactic used by the other person. In this case, you will need to evaluate the reciprocation action and be ready to decline if required.

So how can you use the Reciprocation technique? If you want to influence somebody with this technique, perform an action of reciprocation as described above. In this way, the other party will give it back. Also, if somebody is giving you something or doing something for you, bear in mind that you might have to give or do something back.

Bonding

Next technique under the Connecting category is *Bonding,* a very common technique employed regularly by all of us. I cannot emphasize enough how powerful relationship building (bonding) is in life and in our negotiations. Bonding is building relationships with all parties so that the bonds can help to influence others in negotiations. This is a powerful technique in that it brings a personal touch and frequently helps to ease the negotiation discussions. Forming the bond is an important prerequisite in most negotiations.

Bonding is often created by similarities such as common habits, hobbies, places of origin and associations. A personal experience of mine showcases the importance of associations. In a previous role at work, my job responsibilities included developing and implementing policies. These policies would need to be reviewed with relevant staff members to get their feedback. One such staff member was known to be a tough partner. It was difficult to get him to agree. Having just learned this connecting technique, I did some research and found that we went to the same business school. In my meeting with him, I brought up our association with the business school and talked about it for five minutes. At that point, the discussion took a different turn. Once a connection was established, it became a lot easier to walk him through the policy and get his acceptance.

Have you ever heard of an icebreaker game? When you are in a new class or group, the first agenda item is an icebreaker game. Often this group activity is to introduce yourself, say something unique about yourself or find items common in the group. The goal of such an activity is to build relationships by sharing common hobbies, places and associations.

The most common ways to enhance bonding are by gaining trust, nurturing a relationship, and demonstrating empathy.

- Gaining trust and demonstrating honesty helps toward building a strong connection. In any situation, the moment trust is gained, a solid bond is established. Trust takes a long time to build but can be extremely powerful.

- Nurturing a relationship through constant contact over a period of time is another way to grow stronger bonds. As we have already seen, Reciprocation technique is powerful as it creates the feeling of returning what was previously received. However, when reciprocation happens over and over again, it creates a long-term relationship and converts into Bonding.

- Empathy refers to caring for and connecting with the feelings of another person. Demonstrating empathy and understanding the frame of mind of the other party is useful in improving bonding.

Remember that gaining and keeping trust are very important for maintaining a strong bonding. So, if you make a promise, you would need to fulfill it. As an example, if you agree with your parents for 30 minutes of screen time, add a reminder so that you stick to the promise.

Do you ever feel that a kid or young adult is not easy to talk to, does not engage properly or is emotionally hard to deal with? This happens when with kids or young adults who have certain difficult situations to deal with. The best way to work with such kids or young adults is to engage them on things they like. To build a bond with them, find out what are the topics or activities that serve as a positive outlet for them. Discussing about or helping them engage in these topics or activities helps to build the bond.

I heard a great example about negotiation strategies with kids from a mother. She stated that she always keeps in mind the kids' interests and highlighted an instance where the family was on a guided tour with a lot of walking. A nine-year-old was initially excited but midway through the tour, started getting tired and complaining of aches in different parts of the body. A classic kids' way to get empathy. I asked the mother what was her way of dealing with the situation and convincing the kid to keep going. She mentioned that the best way is to do something fun and make them laugh. So, she starts playing a game as they keep walking. This gets the kid in a positive frame of mind and builds the bond.

How can you use the Bonding technique? You can build great relationships with people either before or during the negotiation using some of the points stated above to influence the other person.

References

The third technique under the Connecting category is References. In this world of ever-increasing options and information overload, references (in the form of reviews, ratings, recommendations, etc.) provide the social support that allows making a decision easier. The use of References is everywhere these days through the growing power of the internet. How many of you rely on reviews as a factor for making a decision? We now live in a world that seems incomplete without the ecosystem of references. Recommendations apply in all sorts of areas such as travel, restaurants, entertainment, movies, jobs and many more. Social marketing uses reviews and recommendations and is now one of the primary methods of marketing.

Some very prominent examples of references are:

- Google's search algorithm providing results based on a ranking derived from the number of page views (a unique form of online reference);

- Google maps, Yelp, TripAdvisor and other sites are used by people to get reviews, and these sites reward users to provide recommendations; and

- Amazon's extraordinary success is due in no small part to its heavy reliance on reviews from other shoppers or users.

References are equally valuable in negotiations. Often while negotiating, the use of references enhances the ability to influence the other person effectively. Don't we often say to our parents, "But Daddy, other kids in my class also have a smart watch. Their parents have allowed it. Why can't I have one?"

Do you remember the story of Adia from Chapter 3? Adia did not want others at the party to watch her video even with all the interest expressed by the guests. Sarah tried all different ways to get Adia to agree. She offered Adia a chocolate and even gave her a glossy lip balm, both of which Adia liked. Though Sarah tried with great determination to use the Reciprocation technique to get agreement, Adia was not to be persuaded to allow the video to be played.

So, Adia's story went on for about 45 minutes at which point everybody was about to give up. Upon watching all this, I decided to jump in and share some information with Sarah that I thought she could use. I called her to the side and said, "In this kind of situation you have to think about what other techniques can be used to convince Adia." I then asked Adia's brother, "Who do you think is one person who Adia likes and listens to most?" He answered, "Her mom!" So, I asked Sarah to go and talk to the mom and ask for her help to convince Adia. I was employing the technique of References. As it turned out, the mom talked to Adia and requested her to agree to play the video. The trick worked! Adia agreed, and we all got a chance to watch the video. It was a fun video and we were amazed by Adia's acting.

Here's another example where the References technique could work effectively. I was walking along with friends in San Francisco when I observed a little girl eating ice cream. Her father was trying different methods to get his daughter to share some of her favorite ice cream. She was, of course, not willing to share with anybody. In this case, how would you get a spoon of ice cream from her?

The father tried different techniques from the array of techniques. First, he tried "Reciprocation" by reminding the girl that he had given her something and that she should now share ice cream with him. That didn't work! Then, he tried to use "Authority" (which we will talk about further ahead) but that didn't work either! At this stage, I thought in my mind that the best and most effective technique he could have used was References. There should be one person that the girl listens to, and in this case, it was her mother. The father could have talked to his wife to ask their daughter to share some ice cream. As can be seen from this story, not all techniques work the same way, and one technique will work better than the others. The various techniques of persuasion have to be understood and applied according to the situation.

References are very valuable in the event of uncertainty. In a negotiation, when there is an element of uncertainty, people look for some kind of assurances that references are able to offer. For example, when a parent is negotiating with a child to go to see a dentist, and is able to mention friends and other kids who have had an enjoyable dental visit.

So, how can you use this technique? Do your research and find out who can be a reference to influence the other person. If the other person is also using a reference, be aware that the technique is being applied. Rely on it only if the reference is somebody in whom you believe or trust. Don't be overly influenced if somebody mentions a celebrity endorsing a product as a reference because it might not make a good decision.

Committing techniques

As the name suggests, these techniques are used to win the other party's commitment. The key while using these techniques is to get the other party onboard and buy in to your point. By doing so, you can then generate a commitment that the other party will feel compelled to fulfil. This category includes two different techniques, Promise and Vested, both of which we all use frequently.

Promise

One of the techniques frequently applied by negotiators is to get a "Promise" from the other person. The promise could be clearly stated or even implied. A clearly-stated promise is provided in written or verbal form whereas an implied promise could be expressed in the form of an action or a strong belief. How many times have you heard or told another person, "But you promised me!" By saying this, you are reminding the other person of a promise they had made and that they need to fulfill. The natural reaction of people is to fulfill promises. In a negotiation, therefore, obtaining a promise early in the discussion helps in securing a commitment from the other person to keep their promise.

Promises or commitments that are written, announced or shared with multiple people generate a stronger binding, and it is recommended to obtain a promise from the other party that is announced or shared widely.

Promises also have the ability to last for a long time. As an example, when two parties enter into a partnership, they each promise to fulfil the commit-ment that can last for a long time.

There are numerous examples in our daily behavior wherein promise is triggered to build a long-term relationship. Google frequently provides free storage or free OS to get a user locked-in for the future. The user promises to continue using the services over the years in response to the benefits Google offers. When negotiating with kids, we often use a combination of Promise and Reciprocation. We often hear parents saying, "If you do this, we will do this...Is that a deal?" By confirming that it is a deal, the parents have given and received a promise.

So, how does promise work in engaging with kids? An experience I had with a three-year-old demonstrates the impact of promise. We visited a friend who had two children, a three-year-old and a seven-year-old. While it was easy to connect with the seven-year-old, it was a bit harder with the three-year-old who was anxious about meeting new people. We tried the old trick of asking for a high-five that often works with most kids. But it did not work. We said she could give us a high-five after she had fun playing with our kids. This created a positive feeling in the way this information was presented and she at least agreed to give us a high-five later. After a while, we checked back with her. I asked her for a high-five and again did not get it easily. She was still shy. At this time, I used the Promise technique. I made a questioning face, and asked, "So you did not have any fun?" and that is why she was not giving me a high-five. Imagine this interaction of influencing a little kid. I asked her the question one more time and this time she gave me a high-five. I asked her if she did have fun and she nodded shyly. Psychology shows that in the end the promise did work.

How can you use the Promise technique? If you get a commitment from the other person, it will drive them to fulfill it. Similarly, if you have promised something, you should fulfill your pledge. This is the rule of promise that can be used to influence the other person.

Vested

This next technique under the Committing category is "Vested". My research and discussions with multiple people have shown that this technique is one of the most commonly used tools for influencing. This technique is useful when the principal objective is to get as many people as possible to agree to an idea or a proposal. The most effective way to achieve consensus on an idea is to agree with individual parties in a negotiation separately prior to the decision being announced or before voting on a proposal. Imagine that your teacher is going to take a vote on which movie to play in your free period in class. If you can discuss and agree with your classmates on one choice, it is likely that the choice you discussed will get the vote when the teacher asks for a decision.

The example of two brothers explains this technique. A few years ago, when Cable TV was newly introduced, an older brother was attracted to it for the movies and shows and wanted to convince his parents to get the subscription. In order to influence a decision from the parents, the older brother first talked to the younger brother separately. He highlighted to his younger brother that the cable TV would stream live cricket from all over the world. By doing this, he convinced the younger brother to support the decision to get a subscription. When it was time to discuss this as a family and arrive at a decision, the chances for a positive outcome were better when both brothers were aligned and united.

You can use this technique in cases where you have to get other people in alignment before a vote or a decision. Talk to the others and gain consensus from them first before the decision is made or voting is taken.

Controlling techniques

The final category of Controlling techniques is used to create an element of control over the other party. The goal is to steer the other party toward an anticipated response. These techniques are Authority, Loss Anxiety and Vividness. Let's now run through each of these.

Authority

We have all used authority as a technique in many of our negotiations. It is the simplest and most intuitive technique to use. Imagine a mother trying to negotiate with a kid, and mentions the name of the father to influence.

Authority refers to a power that a person can get by using facts, expertise, title/position, or rules and regulations to persuade the other person toward taking a specific course of action. Let's see how these are used to generate leverage.

- *Facts* can be used as an important way to get a decision that is made based on solid data and analyses. As an example, by using the data of your good math scores in the class tests, you can influence your parent(s) to get a reward.

- *Expertise* also helps create an influence because an expert carries a reputation that people respect and follow. For example, since the teacher or professor has an expertise in a topic, you can mention the expert's view to influence the other party.

- *Title or Position* are based on the higher standing that gives the power. Title or position could come from a higher rank or wealth. Typically, a parent or grandparent holds a position or rank that can be used to influence the other party.

- Last but certainly not least are *Rules and Regulations* that are considered a strong authority that people are compelled to follow. Have you heard somebody using a law or rule to influence others?

So, how do we deal with situations where the other party used Authority? In some cases, we might not have an option. However, there are ways to respond effectively to the use of authority;

- One way is to counter with another authority. Choose carefully the authority that you use because the other person can use it too.
- Another way is to create innovative and creative solutions that will counter the effect of Authority. Let's take an example to bring this to life.

As we all know, when we talk about a class at school, the professor has the authority. So how do you negotiate with the professor?

A real-life story comes from my class on finance, which was one of the toughest subjects for most of the class. We were negotiating with the professor for a higher grade percentage for class assignments and participation, and a lower percentage for the final exam. Our objective was to reduce the percent score assigned to the final exam to the lowest possible and thereby reduce our stress. However, the professor stated that there was only so much he was allowed to do. He highlighted University rules, another level of authority by which he was governed. Not getting much leeway in terms of the reduction in percentage allocation for the final exam, we asked the professor to consider an open-book final exam. The professor declined that request as well. Finally, one of my classmates came up with a clever idea. It was probably the last-ditch effort in the negotiation. He asked the professor if we could take group exams, and looked around the class to get an affirmation of the idea. Taking his cue, a couple of other classmates jumped in with support for group exams. To the amazement and relief of everybody, our professor agreed with the idea. So, we took the exam in groups of three. At least three minds were better in attempting to tackle a difficult exam problem than taking the exam individually.

Here's another example of creating solutions that mutually work for both. Let's take a situation where your friend owns a set of superhero toys that you are playing with. Since your friend owns the toys, he has the position to make rules. Assume he takes two toys and gives you the other two, but you want to play with all four. In that case, you could come up with solutions that help your objective and, at the same time, keep both of you happy. Some such solutions could be splitting the toys for specific time, trading the superhero toys for something you own that he likes, or playing the superhero toys together.

The Authority technique is easily available and can be put to use in many situations. Bear in mind that the other person can frequently employ it as well. It is important to be aware of situations where the other person applies it and prepare for ways to neutralize the effects by a counter-authority or using innovative solutions.

Loss Anxiety

In this technique, the other party is presented with or highlighted a loss that they might face due to a delayed decision. We see this technique being routinely applied in the process of influencing the other party as it triggers an immediate response caused by the possibility of a loss.

Loss Anxiety arises for the following reasons:

1. Availability loss: The feeling of something that will run out quickly due to limited quantity. I am sure you know how auctions for a rare piece of art create the availability loss through competition. Numerous items are sold as rare or collector's items that will not be available once it is sold. For example, a Black Friday sale that states the availability of only two items at a discounted price demonstrates this well.

2. Urgency loss: The sense of limited time available to make a decision or perform an action to avoid missing the window of opportunity. This technique calls for a quick, impulsive action when it is employed. For example, a sale of tickets for a

popular show that is open for only 24 hours creates the effect of urgency loss.

3. Accessibility loss: The restrictions imposed on the use or access of something to a specified audience thereby creating exclusivity. For example, this is typically used to state that the access or subscription is available only to specific members or is available for a trial period.

This technique is as common and effective in influencing as any other applicable techniques. When I teach negotiation, I advise participants not only to know how to use it but also to be on their guard when others apply this technique.

I want to specifically call out that creating unnecessary fear, threats or any other kind of pressure might work sometimes as a tactic, but it is not a good use of the loss anxiety technique. In my opinion, this tactic attempts to get an upper hand, but it is ineffective and is likely to create distrust.

You can use this technique if you can highlight how the other party can gain a benefit or avoid a loss by making a quick decision.

Vividness

The last and one of the most stimulating techniques frequently used is Vividness. This technique refers to presenting something as very extraordinary to influence the other party toward an expected behavior. The idea is to make an immediate impact that creates a "wow" factor. Vividness comes from distinctive ideas, awe-inspiring videos and other material, analogies, touching the heart, etc.

Disneyland, for example, uses vividness to favorably influence its guests. They use attractive terms to describe common words: employees are called *cast members*, employee interviews are called *auditions*, and customers are called *guests*. This leaves a very special feeling in the mind.

So, how do you influence your dad when you want a beautiful frock you see in the shop? The answer is that you can pass on the message vividly to him. You could talk about how beautiful it is and how nice you would look in it. A friend shared her story when as a young girl she fell in love with a pretty, pink frock in the shop. She kept saying, "It's so beautiful," and "I will look like a doll in that when I dance." Her dad recalled that it was easier to refuse her crying brother for a toy, than to resist her vivid descriptions.

Remember the story about the older brother convincing the younger brother about cable TV? He presented vividly to the younger brother that cricket from all over the world will be streamed live and he would be able to watch his favorite players in action. This made it easy to convince him for the subscription.

Vividness can also come from simplicity. For Google, the vividness of a simple home page captured attention of online visitors due to its minimalist effect. Being one of the most valuable sites on the internet does not compel Google to reconsider its strategy. In the professional world, simplicity is extremely valuable. It is very effective, for example, when communicating a proposal to executives. We frequently need to present complicated processes and proposals to executives, and it is most effective to show it in a simple manner for easier decision-making.

In your negotiations, you can add Vividness as a technique to bring effective results. It leaves an impact on the mind of the other person that could drive the negotiation to successful results.

· · ·

A friend narrated a story of how nicely his son presented an idea about pursuing a degree course in arts and photography to convince his parents. The son had a keen interest in photography, and had the opportunity to use his parents' SLR camera on trips, events and family occasions. He received the title of the "family photographer". The interest in photography generated a passion to pursue it as a long-term profession.

Now, as I mentioned at the start of the influencing techniques section, we all apply some of the techniques on a regular basis. So, it was interesting that the young man used a few of the techniques that we reviewed in this section. Let's look at all the techniques he used:

Reciprocation: He told his parents that he was willing to enroll into a course that his parents suggested but at the same time he would like to join the course in photography.

References: He showed his parents recommendations from friends and other contacts. He worked hard to get these references via phone, email and text, and presented the responses to his parents.

Vested: He convinced his grandparents and other family members to provide the support in the decision as these kinds of decisions were generally discussed as a family.

Vividness: A clever idea he used was to take one of his photographs and put them on covers of magazines as an illustration. It was an extraordinary way to show how he believed his work would be portrayed. He also created video promotions of his photos that presented his photography.

His dedication and passion were very convincing. The parents allowed him to join the course and paid for it too.

Chapter Summary

In this chapter, we discussed the art of negotiation that supports the science of negotiation to make negotiations successful. We started with a review of the behaviors that are essential to a negotiation and then studied the importance of understanding the other party's cultures and styles during the whole negotiation process from preparation to close. We concluded the discussion of the art of negotiation by reviewing the different techniques that are proven to be extremely effective at influencing the other party. After all, we are dealing with people, and appropriate behaviors and application of influencing techniques will help to get the proper response from people.

We have closely followed the story of Rahul's negotiation with his parents for his birthday gift. Let's review the full story next.

WRAP UP:
RAHUL'S BIRTHDAY GIFT

We started Rahul's story by discussing the letter he wrote to his parents summarizing options for his birthday gift (Chapter 1: Introduction)

We looked at how Rahul would be able to apply the WHAM Strategy to present his proposal to his parents (Chapter 3: The Science of Negotiation, "WHAM strategy").

We then discussed the focus on interests and the importance for Rahul to understand both his own interests and those of his parents during the Prepare phase (Chapter 3: The Science of Negotiation, "Interests").

Further, in the Prepare phase, we reviewed how the base level concept works in Rahul's case (Page 15: Base level deal), and discussed the importance for Rahul to identify the alternatives in his negotiation (Chapter 3: The Science of Negotiation, "Alternatives"),

In the Engage phase, we underlined the value for Rahul to confirm his parents' interests and alternatives during the discussion with them. He would also need to build on his interests and alternatives (Chapter 3: The Science of Negotiation, "Engage").

Next, we reviewed how Rahul could present his proposal to his parents to influence them toward a positive mindset. This would help him get a better decision (Chapter 3: The Science of Negotiation, "Presenting your point"). Also, Rahul used the High-value-low value strategy well in his proposal (Chapter 3: The Science of Negotiation, "High value -Low value strategy").

Under Behaviors, we assessed Rahul's style based on details of the case. How could Rahul make the negotiation effective? He would need to adopt a different style (Chapter 4: The Art of Negotiation, "Styles"). Rahul could also have used some of the influencing techniques explained in Chapter 4 "Power of Influencing".

Outcome:
So you must be wondering what the outcome was. In the end, Rahul was offered a one-month subscription for Disney+. When this final gift is proposed by the parents,

Rahul would 1) evaluate if this was the right gift that he wanted, 2) continue to negotiate based on all concepts discussed, or 3) evaluate if he wants to settle for one of his alternatives.

APPENDIX A

NEGOTIATION CHECKLIST

Never go to a negotiation without this!

Check out the checklist on the next page

Also available online at:

www.anujjagannathan.com/negotiation-checklist

CHECKLIST FOR NEGOTIATION PROCESS*

General

- ☐ Evaluate the impact of cultures right through the process
- ☐ Know your style and constraints, and evaluate the impact on negotiations

Prepare

- ☐ Determine what method applies - self-interest or joint-interests
- ☐ Prepare your WHAM strategy to highlight your proposal
- ☐ List your own interests (for joint-interest negotiations)
- ☐ Assess interests of the other party and find mutually beneficial solutions
- ☐ List your alternatives and determine TRAIN
- ☐ Gauge what are the other party's alternatives
- ☐ Prepare for your anchor with justifiable criteria
- ☐ Determine who is the other party's key decision-maker
- ☐ Learn about style of the key decision-maker to customize strategies accordingly
- ☐ Study the culture of the other party, and note the nuances of the cultures
- ☐ Assess techniques that apply, and prepare to apply the technique in the situation
  - ☐ Reciprocation - Are there reciprocation actions that you can call upon to influence?

- Bonding – Can bonding help you derive better solutions?
- References – Identify references you can leverage during negotiations.
- Promise – Are you able to leverage a promise to influence?
- Vested – Incorporate this technique when dealing with multiple stakeholders.
- Authority – Assess the use of authority by either party; find ways to respond to the authority.
- Loss Anxiety – Evaluate the impact of loss anxiety in the negotiation.
- Vividness – Identify ways to present information to make a strong, lasting impact.
- Ascertain all the requirements to a successful closure of the negotiation such as approvals or communication
- Determine any potential conflict matters, and prepare solutions to resolve

Engage

- Build on your interests and theirs through the engagement
- Determine interests of key decision-maker and develop solutions accordingly
- Revisit your list of alternatives; confirm other party's alternatives
- Present your point properly in your engagement

- [ ] Ensure anchors are properly delivered, and carefully handled during the engagement
- [ ] Identify any additional stakeholders that need to be informed or need to approve
- [ ] Ensure that the approvers and signatories are available at close
- [ ] Ensure you earn respect at the table and build trust; demonstrate empathy
- [ ] Use communication essentials
- [ ] Demonstrate confidence and appropriate body language; assess these aspects of the other party to adapt to their behavior
- [ ] Apply techniques assessed during preparation that might work in the situation
- [ ] Decide the level of information exchange based on interactions
- [ ] Walk into the negotiation with optimism and avoid any prior biases (Negoptimism)
- [ ] Do not take "No" as an answer easily. Persist and come up with multiple solutions.
- [ ] Have the courage to ask. This comes from practice.
- [ ] Adapt your style according to the situation, as applicable

Close

- [ ] Complete the agreement on all points
- [ ] Communicate agreement to all relevant parties

- ☐   Determine and agree on the terms of letter or contract if you have to sign one, or on email
- ☐   Ensure all approvals and sign off are obtained
- ☐   Ensure post-signing communication requirements are complete
- ☐   *Refer to chapters for more details on all the checklist points

REFERENCES

Books

Negotiation Quotient by Anuj Jagannathan, 2019

Web

IKEA Story:

East Bay Times, November 14, 2018 "Unique Ikea Store coming to Dublin"

https://www.eastbaytimes.com/2018/11/13/unique-ikea-store-coming-to-dublin/

The Independent, November 15, 2018 "Dublin Approves IKEA Store And Walkable Shopping"

http://www.independentnews.com/news/dublin-approves-ikea-store-and-walkable-shopping/article_0d88829a-e884-11e8-95c4-23e6935eb48a.html

ACKNOWLEDGEMENTS

The support from my family and friends for my first book "Negotiation Quotient: Opening the Door to a Successful Deal" has motivated me to continue writing. My mother, Dr. Neela Jagannathan, and father, Prof. V. R. Jagannathan are both academicians and successful authors. I feel proud to have them as a source of inspiration and continuous support towards accomplishment of this dream.

The first book generated a lot of excitement around the home from my wife, Jyothi Srivathsan and my daughters, Shreya and Nithya. When I mentioned the second book, I got the same reactions. Everybody at home was excited to hear about this book, and the concept. Nithya drew the art for Rahul's story.

Friends and family have helped with the book. Special mention to Shreya and Rishik Buneti who helped to read the manuscript and provided valuable comments from the view of a young reader to improve the content. Some friends and colleagues contributed with experiences of their kids negotiating, and these experiences are stated as examples and cases for the book.

I am grateful for the valuable contributions made by Gary Klinga, a very proficient editor who was not only excellent at editing but also kept ideas flowing as he read the book. His editorial review is below.

"Drawing heavily from his wealth of experience as a finance professional, Anuj Jagannathan offers an in-depth and practical guide for younger minds aspiring to be effective negotiators. Written in a clear and concise manner, We Can Negotiate Too! is a comprehensive handbook covering the essential keys to negotiating a successful outcome, including reciprocity, influencing and style. The book is rich in examples of common challenging situations the young adult will face and how to combine behavioral techniques with effective strategies to skillfully negotiate.

Younger minds will feel better equipped to tackle tomorrow's challenging situations that they will have to face in the business world or in personal relationships. Whether embarking on a professional career for the first time or just building confidence in dealing with challenging day-to-day situations, the trained negotiator steeped in the science of negotiation will be ready and prepared to deal with whatever life throws at them. We Can Negotiate Too! is a valuable resource to have when making smart decisions in the negotiation arena."

ABOUT THE AUTHOR

Anuj Jagannathan is a senior finance professional with over 20 years of experience of dealing with teams, executives, personnel, suppliers, and customers. His rich experience comes from working across diverse industries and in multinational organizations such as Google, Visa, PwC and KPMG. He got his MBA from University of California Los Angeles and National University of Singapore in 2015.

Anuj has a keen passion for the subject of Negotiation. Having completed his MBA in 2015, he has delved deep into the realm of negotiations. Since 2016, he has hosted workshops and webinars on negotiation across the world in diverse organizations from startups to Fortune 500 companies. He has coached participants on negotiating. He received a certificate at the Negotiation and Leadership conference at Harvard Law School in 2017.

In late 2019, he released his first book, an Amazon bestseller "*Negotiation Quotient: Opening the door to a successful deal*" and received 5-star reviews from readers. In less than a year, this is his second book. He is passionate about writing books, blogs and articles. In an effort to help kids and young adults succeed in life, he also hosts webinars or training on negotiation for them.

Connect with the author for any questions, ordering an author-signed copy or to learn more about negotiation training:

LinkedIn: in/anujjagannathan

Website: www.anujjagannathan.com

Email: anuj.email.contact@gmail.com

Please take a few minutes to add a review on Amazon. As an author, I am available to help you in your negotiation journey. Feel free to reach out to me if you have any questions or suggestions. I would be glad to hear from you, my friends!

THANK YOU AND ALL THE BEST!

Made in the USA
Monee, IL
10 March 2022